'Profile's Wonc ... :oming
something of a ... sign, its
scholarly enthu ... pect for the general reader.'
Mark Bostridge, *Independent on Sunday*

'Bradley's perceptive, entertaining and instructive book
… celebrates yet another imaginative leap forward'
Hilary Spurling, *Observer*

'An eloquent, well-illustrated love letter to one of London's
most instantly recognisable landmarks' *London Review of Books*

'This is a brilliant book by the most talented English
architectural topographer of his generation, and a worthwhile
addition to Profile's series of monographs on individual
monumental buildings.' John Martin Robinson, *Literary Review*

'Bradley's constant evocation of the culture of Victorian
railway life is gripping and thorough.' Ken Worpole,
Independent

'Bradley has worked miracles of condensation: there is
nothing in this book that I am not happy to know; much
more of it is valuable to know; all of it is a pleasure to know
… St Pancras is certainly a marvel, but even Bradley's wit,
passion and charm cannot persuade me that Scott's Gothic
wonderhouse ranks with the Parthenon, the Alhambra and
the Taj Mahal. Yet so persuasive a guide is he that I am
prepared to consider that the limitation might be mine, not
the building's.' Judith Flanders, *Spectator*

'A fascinating and detailed tale … there is little more information one could ask of this wondrous place' John McKean, *Architects Journal*

' [Bradley] expounds upon his subject with dazzling breadth and care.' Zoë Strimpel, *FT Magazine*

'*St Pancras Station* is written by an architectural historian; but an architectural historian with a feeling for machinery and an intuitive grasp of planning. It opens up a number of unhackneyed themes for a new and – visually speaking – newly literate readership.' J. Mordaunt Crook, *TLS*

'*St Pancras Station* is a beautifully written book … Simon Bradley's erudition makes it not merely a pleasure to read, but also an excellent introduction to the nineteenth-century Gothic Revival and the great age of railways.' Jeremy Musson, *Country Life*

'The book's importance lies in its clear exposition of the philosophy and stimulus which led to the building of one of our greatest Victorian monuments.' Gordon Biddle, *Railway and Canal Historical Society Journal*

'Well-researched and eclectic … a surprisingly engaging insight into a crucial period of this nation's recent history.' Paul Harrop, *Bookbag*

SIMON BRADLEY is the grandson and great-grandson of engine-men and grew up with a keen interest in railways and railway buildings. In 1994 he joined the staff of the Pevsner Architectural Guides, of which he is now editor. He is the author of two acclaimed volumes in that series, *London 1: The City of London* and *London 6: Westminster*. He lives in London.

WONDERS OF THE WORLD

....

ST PANCRAS STATION

SIMON BRADLEY

PROFILE BOOKS

This paperback edition published in 2007

First published in Great Britain in 2007 by
Profile Books Ltd
3A Exmouth House
Pine Street
Exmouth Market
London ECIR OJH
www.profilebooks.com

5 7 9 10 8 6

Typeset in Caslon by MacGuru Ltd
info@macguru.org.uk
Designed by Peter Campbell
Printed and bound in Great Britain by
CPI Bookmarque, Croydon, CR0 4TD

A CIP catalogue record for this book is available from the British Library.

ISBN 978 1 86197 951 3

Mixed Sources
Product group from well-managed
forests and other controlled sources
www.fsc.org Cert no. TT-COC-002227
© 1996 Forest Stewardship Council

For Clara

CONTENTS

1. St Pancras Station, photographed by Bedford Lemere in the 1890s, before the advent of motor taxis. The Midland Grand Hotel and its approach ramp fill most of the frame. To the left, the train shed can be seen rising behind its screen wall. King's Cross (not shown) stands just beyond, to the right.

GROUNDWORK

Some saints are famous for themselves, others for having things named after them. St Pancras is in the second group: a celebrated railway station that takes its name from a large urban parish, whose ancient, over-restored mother church survives in a dingy corner of inner north London. Ask a taxi-driver for St Pancras's church, and he will probably drive you to its larger successor: a grand Grecian building of 1822 on the Euston Road, the busiest east–west highway of the capital. A little further east, towering over the same highway, is the St Pancras of normal London usage, built in 1867–77 by the Midland Railway Company at the termination of its new trunk route to the capital.

The new station joined the roll-call of famous London termini – Euston, King's Cross, Paddington, Victoria, Waterloo – all of which were likewise built for independent railway companies. A few of these rank among the earliest stations anywhere, opened barely a decade after railways in their mature form first appeared in the industrial north of England. The lines serving them forced their way into the city from every side. Concerned at the destructive effect on the centre of London, the government decreed limits in 1846 beyond which the railways were not allowed to go, and this explains why the companies serving the north and west stopped just north of the Euston Road. Only the underground Metropolitan Railway and its deeper successors (the 'Tube') have come south of this alignment. Even so, the railways' impact on London was profound, as it was on the nation's landscape, industry, patterns of work and leisure, and even on such apparently remote phenomena as advertising, book publishing and branded foodstuffs. Other countries and continents responded differently to the coming of the train, but few were altogether untouched; railways acted as a universal catalyst, accelerating travel, trade and urbanisation, and making possible the control and exploitation of natural resources and colonial empires.

The scale of the terminus at St Pancras suggests something of this wider significance. Its Euston Road frontage measures some 500 feet (150 metres) wide. From south to north, the maximum extent is nearly a thousand feet, a third of a kilometre. Yet the basic form of the Victorian station – and what might be called its split personality – are easily grasped. Its public face is the Midland Grand Hotel, a huge cliff of red brick dressed with stones of different colours: the grandest single monument of the Gothic Revival in Britain. It extends from a square-spired, 240-foot (72-metre) high clock tower at the east end to a lower and bulkier tower towards the west, from which point a curved projection sweeps forward up to the hotel portal. Under this second tower is a giant arch through which departing passengers entered the station proper; an additional arch further east disgorged the arrivals. Apart from the western salient, the hotel building is recessed behind a raised terrace, the front wall of which stands at a slight angle to the main range. The hotel also has a less elaborately treated side range on the west, which runs back aslant

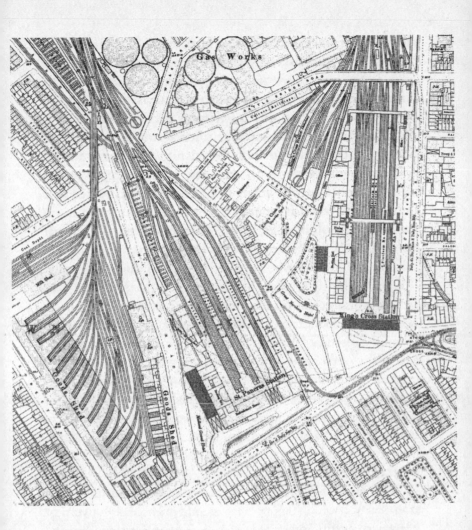

2. The termini at St Pancras and King's Cross on an exquisitely detailed
Ordnance Survey map of 1893. At St Pancras the station hotel is closely
integrated with the trains, at King's Cross it stands to one side. Tracks spill
out of King's Cross to serve added platforms on the left.

along the street called Midland Road. Behind, set end-on to the hotel and effectively concealed from the usual approaches to it, is the enormous iron and glass shelter over the platforms: a structure that in railway parlance is known a little bathetically as a 'train shed'. This rises between screen walls that share the materials and architectural motifs of the hotel, but it is structurally as well as functionally separate from it. The designers were different too: the architect George Gilbert Scott for the hotel and the associated station rooms, the engineer William Henry Barlow for the train shed.

To these could now be added some contemporary designers' names, for St Pancras is entering a new age as the London terminus of the Eurostar services which run via the Channel Tunnel to the Continent. Mighty new works are under way to fit the train shed for this purpose, including a huge boxy extension to shelter longer and more numerous trains. After a long eclipse the Midland Grand is being transformed too, and will reopen after 2007 as a luxury hotel to twenty-first-century standards: quite a coup for an establishment that closed to guests seventy years previously on the grounds of helpless obsolescence. When these works are complete, St Pancras station will once again be what it was in the beginning: the finest and smartest railway station in London, both for travellers and for guests.

Now back to Pancras, the saint: one of the dimmer figures from early church history. His legend tells of a convert of Phrygian origin, martyred at the age of fourteen in the Emperor Diocletian's persecutions in early fourth-century Rome. The historical Pancras may never have existed at all; none the less, in 630 a substantial church was built around his reputed tomb on the Aurelian Way, just outside the walls of Rome. In the same century England too acquired at least one church dedicated to him, built in Canterbury following Pope Gregory the Great's initiative to convert the heathens of the island. This mission of Roman monks landed in 597, probably at Ebbsfleet in Kent, carrying relics of the saint. London was then in East Saxon territory, where the king was less favourable to Christianity than his counterpart in Kent. So Canterbury became the ecclesiastical capital instead, and London remained without a bishopric or a cathedral until early in the next century.

Daughter churches followed, of which our St Pancras is traditionally among the earliest. A seventh-century date has been claimed, on the basis of an incised altar slab discovered here in 1847. Unsporting scholars have since pointed out that the same type of slab was current until the fourteenth century, and that no part of the standing fabric can be dated to before about 1100. But this does not disprove an older origin, perhaps in the form of a timber church. An ancient lineage is certainly suggested by the outlandish dedication, and perhaps also by the location outside the walls of the old Roman city – as at St Pancras in Canterbury, and San Pancrazio in Rome itself.

Many centuries passed before the growing capital began to encroach on the land of St Pancras parish. By late Georgian times burials were increasingly frequent, the architect Sir John Soane and the feminist Mary Wollstonecraft among them. To fit them all in, the churchyard had to be enlarged repeatedly before final closure to interments in the 1850s. Then in summer 1866 it was abruptly curtailed in its south-east corner, behind a large timber hoarding of exceptional height. Much of what was dug up behind this enclosure was removed with extreme care. Another peculiarity was that work did not stop after dusk, but went on by the light of flare lamps.

These fragile excavations were of human remains, of course, for the corner in question lay right in the path of the Midland Railway's new route. Trial diggings for the work had been mismanaged. The Vicar of St Pancras noted skulls and thigh-bones scattered heedlessly about, and complained to the Bishop of London, who prevailed on the Home Secretary to stop it. The railway company then engaged a well-regarded architect called Arthur Blomfield – the son of the late Bishop of London, no less – to oversee the exhumations. Blomfield's practice was to drop in unexpectedly at the site, to ensure that the clerk of works was not cutting corners. To be doubly sure, he also set one of his pupils to watch the excavations, a 26-year-old Dorset man named Thomas Hardy.

Young Thomas Hardy usually visited at around five or six in the evening. He checked that any coffins still intact were being raised correctly on planks, and that cadavers whose coffins had disintegrated under the shovel were properly re-boxed. One such coffin turned out to contain a full skeleton and an extra skull (clearly a two-headed man, Blomfield later joked to Hardy). Other interments lay as loose bones in the boggy ground, described not long before as 'saturated with decomposition'. These too were gathered and respectfully reinterred. When work finished in 1867, an estimated eight thousand dead Londoners had been relocated, either else-where within the churchyard, to new suburban cemeteries such as Highgate or Kensal Green, or even – for reasons that will become clear – off to France.

Hardy's biographers speculate how far this gruesome business may have deepened the writer's tendency to see the

3. St Pancras train shed under construction, engraved for the *Illustrated London News*, 15 February 1868, from a viewpoint just south of the churchyard. The timber scaffolding will shortly move forward to allow work to begin on the next of the arches, the stubs of which are already in place. The giant half-buried pipe carries the once-notorious Fleet sewer.

skull beneath the skin of life. These months were certainly crucial for his future course: his religious faith ebbed, his health faltered and soon afterwards he returned to Dorset, where he abandoned architecture to live by his pen. But Hardy's five-year pupillage in London was also a time of exciting exploration; forty years later he recalled with relish 'strolling up and down Holborn Hill before the Viaduct was constructed, wandering in the labyrinth of Seven Dials before the new Avenues were cut'. To which he might have added, walking in Agar Town: for this slum district south of the churchyard was levelled and erased to build St Pancras station. Such convulsions were widespread in the 1860s to 1870s, as the Victorians strove to modernise the capital of the greatest empire the world had yet seen. The Metropolitan Railway dates from these years – it runs just beneath the carriageway of the Euston Road – as do many celebrated thoroughfares: Holborn Viaduct, Shaftesbury Avenue, Victoria Embankment, Queen Victoria Street, Charing Cross Road.

The new architecture along these streets was puny by comparison with St Pancras, however. In the words of its twentieth-century historian Jack Simmons: 'The station distils the very essence of Mid-Victorian power: for it is the most magnificent commercial building of the age, reflecting more completely than any other its economic achievement, its triumphant technology, its assurance and pride, suffused by romance.' Part of the station's magic is the way in which it illustrates two different approaches to building, held in creative tension: architectural design founded on style and association at the magnificent Neo-Gothic hotel and the pure expression of structure and function at the vast soaring train shed (though this dichotomy may be something of an over-simplification, as we shall see).

Now this greatest of High Victorian secular buildings is set to win further allure as the nation's most prestigious railway terminus. The Channel Tunnel works need extra land, and so St Pancras's churchyard has been dug up again, this time with archaeologists in attendance to record and study the burials and skeletons beneath. Among those exhumed and examined have been senior French clergy driven from their country by the Revolutionary regime after 1792, the co-religionists of those exiles whose bones were repatriated in the 1860s. Many of these refugees found homes in Somers Town, the quarter west of old Agar Town. Arthur Dillon, Archbishop of Narbonne and Primate of Languedoc, was interred complete with his gold-sprung false teeth of best porcelain. Other excavated bones include those of Maurice Margarot, a revolutionary sympathiser sentenced to transportation from Scotland to Australia in 1792, who returned only to die in the local workhouse in 1815. So the bones of revolutionary and archbishop, with other jumbled skeletons English and French, have been re-exiled to a suburban cemetery in order to help speed the journey between Britain and France.

These posthumous ironies would doubtless have been enjoyed by Hardy, whose own hours with the coffins and flare-lamps sounded their after-echoes in a poem of 1882, 'The Levelled Churchyard':

> We late-lamented, resting here,
> Are mixed to human jam,
> And each to each exclaims in fear,
> 'I know not which I am!' ...

Where we are huddled none can trace,
And if our names remain,
They pave some path or porch or place
Where we have never lain!

Hardy's eye for the turning wheel of fortune might well have gleamed at some other vicissitudes in the station's history. There is the sorry tale of George Gilbert Scott junior, the gifted but wayward architect son of the Midland Grand Hotel's great designer. After years of alcoholic vagrancy, scandalous sexual misconduct and intermittent lunacy the younger Scott ended up as one of the hotel's long-term residents. As he lay dying in 1897 the children he had barely known visited to make their farewells, climbing the dizzying staircase of their grandfather's masterpiece. Four decades after, the hotel that had once been the smartest in London was considered so antiquated and unprofitable that it was turned into humdrum railway offices. In 1948 ownership passed to the people, in the form of the nationalised British Railways. That body showed its appreciation of architecture by proposing in 1966 to dispose of the station and divert its trains elsewhere, only to be foiled by another representative of the people, the Ministry of Housing and Local Government, which promoted the building to the highest grade of protection on the national list. British Rail (as it became) then decided to be proud of St Pancras instead, taking out full-page newspaper advertisements in the 1970s to say as much – a volte-face nicely skewered in the pages of *Private Eye*.

The station continued working efficiently through all these uncertainties, but usage of the hotel for offices ceased altogether in the late 1980s. By the turn of the millennium the

Some people would demolish it.

In fact, that's just what British Rail wanted to do, ten years ago.

Only they weren't allowed to, by the GLC Historic Buildings Board.

Apparently a lot of long-haired sentimentalists like Sir John Betjeman thought there was something special about this horrible, tatty old Victorian pile.

Even now, if we wanted to knock it down, these faceless bureaucrats wouldn't let us.

In fact we've got hundreds of these ghastly old relics, dotted about the country.

We've been trying to knock most of them down and sell them to property speculators for years.

In some cases we even managed to slip it through — look at those wonderful new office blocks that Richard Seifert has just put up where the Euston Arch used to stand.

But as for the rest of all this so-called architectural heritage — we're lumbered with it.

So we've decided to do the next best thing, by spending thousands of pounds taking ludicrous advertisements all over the place claiming that we care passionately about these wonderful gems of British culture — in the hope that a few idiots might be gulled into thinking that Sir Peter Parker is a deeply sensitive figure, similar to Lord Clark of Civilisation.

 **British Rail**

Only to be used in case of emergency

4. Slogan and image come from a genuine British Rail advertisement, the rest is *Private Eye* (4 August 1978).

[11]

pathos of neglect inside was extreme. Paintwork was crazed and blistering, hanging frond-like from ceilings, or scattered in slivers across bare-boarded floors; wires sagged and spooled out of makeshift trunking and down begrimed walls; a film of gritty dust lay on every light-bleached window sill; tatty, ill-matched office furniture sat abandoned in odd corners. Some of the rooms – the hotel has over 400 of them – retained un-hotel-like labels such as 'Food Technology', recalling the long occupancy of the state-owned British Transport Hotels' headquarters. Trial patches on walls and ceilings showed where conservators had scraped off paint layers to reveal strata of complex stencilled decoration surviving beneath. Unheated for years, the tiled floors, stony doorways and metal balustrades took on a chill that in winter became mortifying. The effect was eerie, in places even sinister; but the survival of almost every key feature of the Victorian design also made a visit strangely inspiring: the hotel would surely awake from its coma one day.

In eclipse the hotel became one of London's weirder visitor attractions. Weekend parties were conducted round until the last weeks of 2005, paying £5 for a tour lasting an hour or more. During London's Open House weekend, when free entry is granted to buildings normally inaccessible to the public, a long and patient queue would snake along the Euston Road. Some guides liked to warn visitors of the hotel's ghost, a man glimpsed going up the stairs who can never be found afterwards. Less intangible relics of the past, gathered from old cupboards or under floorboards, were exposed in glass-topped display cases in the final room on the circuit: collapsed packets of pre-king-size Player's Navy Cut and Wild Woodbine cigarettes; an archaic playing card, square-

5. A first-floor corridor in the Midland Grand, photographed in 2004 shortly before work began to return it to hotel use.

cornered and numeral-less; an early and lethal-looking electric hairdryer; a gnarled pair of leather boots.

More recent traces – a blue sequin in the corner of a room, fragments of a feather boa drifting across a draughty landing – betrayed opportunistic incursions for fashion shoots or experimental theatre performances. Other temporary residents included film-makers, whose inventive transformations of the dilapidated spaces can be seen in *Chaplin* (1992, Robert Downey Jr), *Richard III* (1995, Ian McKellen), *From Hell* (2001, Johnny Depp), or *Batman Begins* (2005, Christian Bale) to give four examples among many. The action of the Spice Girls' first video, 'Wannabe' (1996), also takes place here, mercifully disguised with heavy drapes and hangings. The exterior has been captured too, across a wider timespan: immortally as a leitmotif in Alexander McKendrick's *The Ladykillers* (1955), where it closes the view from the widow's house in which Alec Guinness's absurd robber gang self-destructs; more balefully in Mike Leigh's *High Hopes* (1988), where it looms over a naïve runaway's arrival in London; most cheekily in *Harry Potter and the Philosopher's Stone* (2002), to represent the exterior of the much less cinegenic King's Cross station immediately alongside.

When Continental services begin in 2007, St Pancras will move from the margins back to the centre of the life of the capital. Brussels and Paris will become about as near in journey time as the Midland city of Leicester was when the building was completed back in 1876. After a good view of Old St Pancras Church, departing passengers will be carried to the tunnel via a new high-speed line passing through Ebbsfleet, the very place in Kent where the papal mission is thought to have landed back in 597. A change of train or two in France will allow travellers to proceed to Termini station in Rome, from which a moderate walk south-west and across the Tiber will bring them to the tomb of St Pancras (one wonders how many modern pilgrims will make the trip). On the way the train passes through the heartlands of medieval Europe, the well-spring of inspiration for Scott's Neo-Gothic hotel, whose astonishing towered and pinnacled skyline still catches the eye and thrills the imagination of the explorer of London.

GOING GOTHIC

The frontage of St Pancras is Gothic. That is to say, it adopts the architectural style of western Europe during the later Middle Ages, a way of building pioneered in the greater churches of France during the twelfth century and characterised in its fullest form by pointed arches, ribbed stone vaults of pointed profile, and flying buttresses. There are no flying buttresses at the hotel, it is true, and not that many rib-vaulted spaces, but the arrays of pointed-arched openings, the spiky pinnacles and the steepling roofs unmistakably signal its derivation from the Age of Chivalry.

That something as new and up-to-date as a railway terminus hotel should speak the architectural equivalent of the language of Dante or Chaucer is ostensibly bizarre. More paradoxical still, the international movement known as the Gothic Revival found its fullest and finest expression not in some obscurantist backwater but in nineteenth-century Britain, the most powerful and economically advanced country in the world. To resolve this apparent contradiction it is best to start with its architect, George Gilbert Scott.

THE WORKING LIFE OF GEORGE GILBERT SCOTT

Scott's life was driven by staggering energy and a limitless appetite for work. In this he recalls other great Victorians such as Dickens, born a year after him in 1812, or Gladstone, born two years before in 1809. The number of projects between 1833, when the fledgling architect designed a rectory for his clergyman father, and Scott's death in 1878, has been estimated variously at between eight hundred and over a thousand. Churches and church or cathedral restorations made up a high proportion, but his portfolio also bulged with ministerial headquarters, hospitals, college and university buildings, town halls, baths, prisons, mansions, town houses, parsonages and cottages. To which must be added the Albert Memorial, the work for which he was knighted in 1872 (rather confusingly as 'Sir Gilbert Scott'), and of course the Midland Grand Hotel. These works are distributed throughout the country; of all the English and Welsh counties only Cardiganshire is Scott-free. He designed for lands beyond the sea too, with major buildings in Germany, Newfoundland, India, Australia and New Zealand, placing him among the earliest architects with a truly global reach.

Such a workload was feasible only by delegation, so Scott pioneered the development of a house style in which pupils and assistants could work confidently and consistently from outline sketches handed down from above. This was just as well, for the boss was often too busy to look at their work at all. His pupil T. G. Jackson recalled the office in the early 1860s, when it contained the then extraordinary total of twenty-seven staff:

I have seen three or four men with drawings awaiting correction or approval grouped outside his door. The door flew open and out he came: 'No time today!' The cab was at the door and he was

6. George Gilbert Scott, in a photographic *carte de visite* of the 1860s.

whirled away to some cathedral where he would spend a couple of
hours and then fly off again to some other great work at the other
end of the kingdom. Now and then the only chance of getting
instructions was to go with him in the cab to the station.

Humorous tales were related of the consequences of
Scott's over-production. He visits a church in the course of
erection, points out various faults to its clerk of works and is
gently redirected to the right church, further down the same
road. He asks admiringly after another church glimpsed from
the train, only to be told that it is his own. Turning up at
the office as usual, his pupils find a plaintive telegram sent
by their earlier-rising master on arriving at some midlands
station: 'Why am I here?' It is perfectly possible that all these
stories are true; certainly Scott exploited train travel for all it
was worth, and the way in which the railway network grew
and changed almost monthly must have been disorientating
in ways we can now hardly imagine. But in some respects
Scott's practice now seems less phenomenal than it did to his
contemporaries, especially in the use of a studio style and in
the readiness to work beyond national boundaries, like such
contemporary globe-trotting architects as Norman Foster
or Frank Gehry – for Scott was as close to a 'brand' as the
Victorian architectural profession would ever get.

Lesser men might have used the hours left over from
design work, client meetings and site visits for socialising or
relaxation. Scott seems hardly to have relaxed at all, except
when laid low by illness, more than once brought on by
stress or overwork. Instead, he wrote and illustrated several
books, produced sheaves of articles, papers and reports, co-
founded an architectural museum and a sketching society,

gave professorial lectures at the Royal Academy, and served a two-year term as president of the Royal Institute of British Architects. He also found time to marry his cousin, to father five sons, training two of them as architects, and to tour the Continent repeatedly on sketching expeditions or in connection with his own projects there. Scott would later rebuke himself for neglecting his family; even when he managed to join them on their long seaside holidays he was apt to spend the day working out his latest designs in giant tracings in the sand.

Thousands of waking hours were also devoted to church and to private prayer, for Scott remained profoundly religious throughout his life, and more concerned with inner states than outward show. Jackson remembered his 'negligent dress and ill-brushed hat ... counterbalanced by a certain unconscious dignity in his manner'. Memoirs and obituaries concur that he was held in high regard and general affection, though he was too modest and reserved for either intimate friendship or gregarious fun. Drawn and painted portraits give him a Gladstonian aspect, with high-domed, intellectual forehead and side-whiskers (rather than a full, Bohemian beard). In photographs he appears less like a great statesman and more like, say, a senior civil servant. Scott's self-image may have been closer to that on the memorial brass on his tomb at Westminster Abbey, where his restoration work had been a source of special pride. Here he appears as the perfect medieval Victorian, framed within a Gothic arch and diligently drawing up a church plan. The funeral itself was akin to a state occasion: thirty-eight carriages followed the coffin, one of them sent by the Queen herself.

Scott's career also reflects, to a remarkable degree, the

7. A detail of Scott's tomb-slab at Westminster Abbey, designed by his star
pupil, the Neo-Gothic architect George Edmund Street. The great architect
is framed by his favourite thirteenth-century forms. The complete slab
includes much larger figures of a medieval architect and a knight in armour
standing guard by a crucifix.

changing shape of architectural patronage and culture during his lifetime. We know a great deal about it thanks in particular to his autobiography, the first by any British architect to be published. The text, mostly pencilled into leather-bound notebooks between 1864 and 1877 during Scott's endless peregrinations by train, is itself a by-product of the railway age. Begun as a private record for his sons, the manuscript includes much on matters of faith and family, including some deeply affecting pages on the deaths of his wife and his third son. Most of this was excised from the posthumously published version of 1879, entitled *Personal and Professional Recollections*. (Its editor was Scott's eldest son, George Gilbert Scott junior, the same who later died insane in the Midland Grand Hotel – often called 'Middle Scott', to distinguish him from his father and from his own son Sir Giles Gilbert Scott, the architect *inter alia* of Liverpool Cathedral, Battersea and Bankside power stations, and the familiar red K2 and K6 telephone boxes. Even architectural historians sometimes muddle the three G. G. Scotts, and in its confusion the Midland Railway's own *Official Guide* invented a phantom fourth, 'Sir Gilbert G. Scott'.) Strenuously fair-minded where others are concerned, Scott's tone veers about dramatically when he himself is the subject: sometimes acutely defensive, sometimes laceratingly self-critical, sometimes naïvely self-regarding. The last of these moods can make irksome reading: Scott tells us, for example, that his church at Camberwell (1841) was 'the best church by far which had then been erected', that a set of drawings (1856) was 'perhaps, the best ever sent in to a competition, or nearly so'; that the St Pancras hotel 'is often spoken of to me as the finest building in London; my own belief is that it is possibly *too good* for its purpose' (a passage that proved irresistible to detractors). So Scott springs from peak to peak of his mountainous achievements, pausing now and again to look ruefully down into the chasms of professional failure and disappointment. But no other Victorian architect could have written in quite this way, for none could boast such a range and variety of work.

THE LONG GOTHIC REVIVAL

Nearly all of Scott's buildings are Gothic. In England, at least, this quintessential style of the Middle Ages was 'revived' even before it had properly died. There were compelling reasons for this reluctance to break absolutely with the past. The Anglican Church, though Protestant, preserved a hierarchy of bishops and archbishops and their cathedrals each with its dean and chapter, just as in the Middle Ages. Nearly all the parish churches were wholly or partly Gothic too, as were the quasi-monastic colleges of Oxford and Cambridge in which the clergy were educated. On the secular side, crown, law and Parliament also originated during the medieval centuries. The English ruling classes therefore liked to trace their ancestry back before the Reformation, and to display and validate it in the medieval language of heraldry. As early as the first Queen Elizabeth's time the aristocracy also built self-consciously chivalric palaces such as Wollaton and Hardwick Hall, inspired by the traditions of medieval romance. This Neo-Gothic consciousness faded somewhat in the later seventeenth and eighteenth centuries, but even the new breed of professional architect – Wren, Hawksmoor, and Robert Adam included – proved ready to turn out neo-medieval designs in order to evoke the native past. A tradition of Gothic architecture, however approximate in details and motifs, thus survived the passing of the living techniques inherited from the Middle Ages.

Some of the most revealing of these 'Gothick' commissions were undertaken by the landed classes for their own domains. One celebrated example is Strawberry Hill, a Thames-side villa remodelled from the 1750s for the socialite and man of letters Horace Walpole, as a strange mixture of scrupulously replicated Gothic features, antiquarian bric-à-brac and high-camp allusions to imaginary monks and cardinals. Here, by stained-glass window-light, Walpole wrote *The Castle of Otranto* (1764), the founding example of the so-called Gothic novel. Its apparatus of castle dungeons, repressive authority and sexual menace provided the stock-in-trade for fiction up to Bram Stoker's *Dracula* (1897) and beyond, and on into the world of Hammer and Hollywood (the true line of descent of the black-clad modern Goths, the sunlight-averse post-punk youth cult). There was a heavy measure of posturing in all this, but Gothic was also used with entire seriousness of purpose. Take the strange triangular Gothic Temple of the 1740s at Lord Temple's gigantic landscape garden at Stowe, Buckinghamshire, with its portal lettered after a French historical tragedy: 'I thank God that I am not a Roman'. The inscription has been read as a jibe at the Catholic Church of Rome; yet the main mansion at Stowe is sternly Roman, as are most of the other temples – the play on the patron's name was deliberate – that embellish the grounds. The wider implication of the Gothic Temple is therefore that old English liberties and ancient Roman and Greek virtues should be harmoniously interfused.

This openness to the construction of meanings helps to

8. The triangular Gothic Temple at Stowe (1742), one of the first Neo-Gothic buildings that Scott encountered. Though seriously meant, by Victorian standards of archaeological accuracy it was a ludicrous performance.

explain the continuing success of the Gothic Revival, which by the late eighteenth century had become an accepted ingredient of educated taste. Not only did Gothic buildings represent values and associations that remained imaginatively alive in the present; contemporaries loved to debate and analyse their 'Picturesque' aspects too. They were sketched in countless amateur drawings and watercolours, and circulated in the form of engravings, vignettes and keepsakes.

Ancient buildings then acquired extra semantic depth once the French Revolution declared a new start for humanity, grounded in universal rights. In response, the older societies of Europe clung defensively to their inheritance from the monarchical, aristocratic and ecclesiastical past. (The penniless French nobility and refugee clergy who fled to sanctuary in Britain – Archbishop Dillon of St Pancras's churchyard among them – were now received as allies rather than as the old foes of roast beef and Protestant liberty.) More than this, the revolutionary wars that tore the Continent between 1793 and 1815 made it dangerous for Britons to venture abroad at all. Deprived of stimulus from Paris *à la mode* and from Mediterranean antiquity, fashionable culture – architecture included – became markedly more introverted and patriotic. New churches and great houses, building types with a clear medieval ancestry, began to adopt medieval dress. Even George III's short-lived palace at Kew, begun in 1801, imitated the outlines of a late medieval fortress.

Meanwhile debate flourished as to the origin of the Gothic style, usually taking the pointed arch as its defining feature. Lack of access to foreign examples for study proved no obstacle to patriotic medievalists, who tried to show that English Gothic churches were variously the earliest, or the purest, or the finest, or all three. New names for the style came into favour: 'Pointed', 'Christian', even 'English' – anything but 'Gothic', a derogatory label inherited from Renaissance Italy, which scapegoated the invading Goths for the supposed impurities of medieval architecture. But origins and labels counted for less in the end than the consensus that Gothic was a fully naturalised and patriotic style, at home in the landscape and the settlements from which it had sprung.

By the time peace returned to Europe, Neo-Gothic design was therefore more entrenched than ever in the British Isles. It also began to spread across the restored monarchies of the Continent: to the German states, where the Middle Ages had been a touchstone of cultural resistance to the French invader; to France itself, where its legitimist and Catholic associations chimed in with the restored Bourbon dynasty; and to Belgium, where it bolstered the patriotic Catholicism that had galvanised resistance to Dutch annexation. Each of these lands had splendid buildings of its own to serve as models, harnessing architecture to the nationalist sentiments that would dominate the rest of the century.

This was the world into which Scott was born, four years before the final act of the Napoleonic wars at Waterloo. The blessings of the peace that followed seemed uncertain in Britain, where poverty, unemployment and unrest raised fears of home-grown revolution. Counter-measures included planting new state-funded churches, where respect for the laws and powers of the land could be drummed into the swelling urban population. Though the extravagant church for St Pancras parish was strictly Grecian, the bulk of these new foundations were Gothic. Meanwhile, understand-ing of Gothic forms and periods was growing all the time, especially in scholarly and antiquarian circles. But this was only one shade in the spectrum of neo-medievalism, which in its popular forms was both strongly literary and markedly plural. In the forefront were the vivid historical novels and chivalric ballads of Sir Walter Scott, a Scottish borderer and Tory. These entranced younger writers such as the politically radical London poet John Keats, who in turn conjured an alternative past of erotic yearning, as in 'The Eve of St Agnes', where rosy light falls on the heroine's bosom beneath 'a casement high and triple-arched ... all garlanded with carven imageries'. In short, Romantic medievalism had something to offer to almost everyone. Reclaimed from specialists and literalists, the Middle Ages became an imaginative playground open to all – rather like Outer Space in twentieth-century science fiction (at least for the male half of the public).

Popular medievalism also enhanced the appeal of Gothic to those who were already susceptible on more conventional church-and-state grounds. It was a faction of MPs and peers of just this type who seized control of the rebuilding competition after the Houses of Parliament burned down in 1834. They stipulated that designs should be Gothic or Elizabethan only: the strongest signal yet that medievalism had become a signifier of national identity. This, the greatest architectural commission in nineteenth-century Britain, was won by Charles Barry and A. W. N. Pugin, whose design took until 1868 to complete: the same year in which the first trains ran into St Pancras. The station frontage building has a certain affinity with the new Palace of Westminster, with its asymmetrical plan dominated by balanced but non-matching towers. But in detail, and thus in connotation and association, the two are quite different, for the red-brick and coloured-stone Gothic of St Pancras evokes Flanders, France and Italy rather than Old England. Something had happened between the 1830s and the 1860s to fracture the home-grown associations of Gothic, which had sustained its revival through the previous centuries. This break with its own continuities is the single most fascinating episode in the Gothic Revival, and the greatest test of its powers of self-renewal. Once again, Scott's own career is central to the wider story.

SCOTT AND THE GOTHIC

The leitmotif of Scott's *Recollections* is the quest for the true Gothic. Scott found his way into its revival haphazardly, from a mixture of personal enthusiasm and wider trends in taste and patronage. A quasi-religious conversion to Gothic in 1840 initiated a deeper engagement that would continue to the end of his life.

This irregular trajectory was not unique, given that the usual training of an architect up to the 1840s was entirely in the classical tradition. The normal path was a four-year pupillage to an established practitioner, which might be supplemented by public lectures and drawing lessons. Scott's architectural education was orthodox in these respects, but in other ways it was distinctly odd. His father, a country vicar in Buckinghamshire, could not afford to send all his sons to school, but George did at least receive lessons from a Mr Jones, drawing master. The two sometimes met at one of the local churches, which Scott loved to delineate in every detail. The *Recollections* present this interest as wholly personal and spontaneous, but we have seen how far the passion for things

[29]

medieval had become general by the 1820s. It is likely, then, that Scott simply picked up a local strain of the general infection; he certainly never forgot his early visits to the ('ludicrous') Gothic Temple at nearby Stowe.

This precocious interest suggested to the vicar that architecture might provide his son with a career. And so the fourteen-year-old Scott was packed off to stay with his learned uncle the Revd Samuel King, who instructed him in mathematics, mechanics, trigonometry and the rudiments of classical building. Meanwhile his father searched for a suitable architect whose office Scott might enter, which in practice meant one whose beliefs corresponded with his own Low Church convictions. He duly chose James Edmeston of Homerton, north London, safely Evangelical in religion but in artistic terms barely more than a hack. (Edmeston's best-known work is not a building, but the hymn 'Lead us, Heavenly Father, lead us'.)

Here Scott learned the basics of the building world, using his spare time for sketching tours and self-improvement. Two useful but uncreative years followed this pupillage, at first working with building contractors, then as assistant and draughtsman to the very capable Henry Roberts, another classically inclined architect. Late in 1834 Scott moved to the office of Sampson Kempthorne, who had recently landed the plum post of architect to the new Poor Law Commission. The English Poor Law had just been reformed on more institutional lines: paupers and the infirm now had to enter a workhouse to receive food and shelter, rather than being paid a small dole for subsistence. New workhouses were therefore needed in quantity, for which Kempthorne provided both model designs and plans for specific sites. Quite a few of these workhouses have survived the eclipse of the Poor Law system, usually after mutating into ordinary hospitals, and very harsh and austere buildings they are too. But in the event Scott's stint in Kempthorne's workhouse-mill lasted only two months, for the death of his father forced him to set up in practice on his own early in 1835.

What happened next – a source of some embarrassment in Scott's later life – was that he became a kind of hack architect himself, and a specialist in the despised workhouse genre at that. In order to establish himself securely he also had to work frantically hard. He was joined in this toil by an even younger architect, a Cornishman named William Bonython Moffatt, formerly his fellow pupil in Edmeston's office. Over the next decade the pair produced some fifty workhouses, about 15 per cent of the national total. From 1838 to 1845 they were in formal partnership, which foundered on Moffatt's unstable, over-confident character: Scott's memoirs record 'absolutely wild' speculations in railway shares, and that Moffatt 'used to boast that he could *afford* to make a fool of himself'. But at first all went well. The two would visit a coffee-house every week to see the country papers and sniff out new workhouse competitions. Designs were often made overnight, and much of the necessary travelling was nocturnal too, the bulk of it on horseback or by coach rather than on the embryonic railway system. Commissions for comparably grim institutional buildings soon followed, including the new county gaol at Reading, one of several Neo-Tudor designs among the classical multitude.

Connections established in these works led to increasing numbers of church commissions, which rapidly became the staple diet of the office. By the late 1830s the burning question in church architecture was no longer the choice between classical and Gothic, but how far to reproduce medieval forms convincingly, both in detail and in general outline. Advanced taste increasingly restricted the ideal models to the century or so either side of 1300, which was considered to have struck the best balance between early Gothic austerity and the all-over enrichment, perpendicular outlines and flatter silhouettes of later centuries. Two very different authorities, both self-appointed, did most to establish this agenda: the young Roman Catholic architect A. W. N. Pugin and the Cambridge Camden Society.

We have already met Augustus Welby Northmore Pugin as co-author of the Palace of Westminster, where the interiors are detailed almost entirely to his designs. A year younger than Scott, Pugin was still more precocious and worked even more frenetically hard, only to die at the age of forty, exhausted and insane, in 1852. His father was one of the French Royalist refugees of the 1790s, who reinvented himself in London as an architectural draughtsman, specialising in the increasingly popular surveys of Gothic buildings. Young Augustus inherited his graphic skills and his medievalism, which soon turned into an obsession. In 1835 he converted to Roman Catholicism, convinced that Gothic could only be revived fully and truthfully within a Christian society reborn on medieval lines. His first book was *Contrasts* (1836), a series of brilliant and cruelly unfair pictorial comparisons between late medieval England and his own day, presented respectively as a golden age of art, faith and charity and a hell of exploitation and indifference directed from mean, shoddy and pretentious buildings. Scott must have flinched in particular at the 'Contrasted Residences for the Poor': above, a

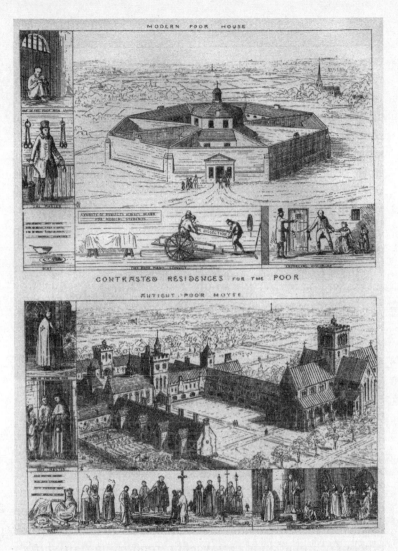

9. Past and present residences for the poor, according to Pugin's *Contrasts* (1836). Modern miseries represented include the removal of pauper cadavers for medical dissection, a final indignity of workhouse existence.

brand-new workhouse, with vignettes including a bleak cell interior and the master brandishing whip and shackles; below, the splendid St Cross Hospital at Winchester, bordered by scenes of medieval charity and pious communal life.

Pugin's Catholicism would restrict the scale and budgets of his independent architectural works, but his influence in other ways was immense. Designs for plausibly medieval-looking fittings and furniture flowed unceasingly from his desk, and leading manufacturers changed their ways and transformed their catalogues in order to realise them. His buildings and writings were also scrutinised intensely by those who shared his love of 'Pointed' architecture. Pugin's understanding of the nature of Gothic soon crystallised into a coherent argument in favour of its intrinsic truth, set out in 1841 in his most important book, *The True Principles of Pointed or Christian Architecture*. This begins with some cardinal rules, all of which Pugin derived from Gothic: that '*there should be no features about a building which are not necessary for convenience, construction, or propriety*'; that ornament should always enrich the essential construction; that every detail 'should *have a meaning or serve a purpose*'; and that every design should be adapted to its material. From here it is only a short step to the axiom of twentieth-century Modernism, that form follows function, always and everywhere.

As a comprehensive account of how medieval builders thought and worked, the *True Principles* were nonsense, for the Middle Ages actually revelled in the imitation of one medium by another: England's cathedrals abound in timber versions of stone vaults, extravagant stone vaults derived from timber ceilings, and stone tombs and shrines scaled up from smaller versions in metalwork. But in practice these inconsistencies counted for little, any more than Pugin's sectarian insistence that truthful design could be achieved only by faithful Catholics limited his audience to members of that church. For Pugin's writings made everything beautifully simple. To anyone whose sympathies were already medieval he enrobed Gothic in a moral superiority above and beyond mere associations with religious faith. The architecture of the future was the architecture of the past. It was on the side of God, and vice versa. Everything else, and everyone else, was wrong.

The Anglican faction which came closest to sharing these ideals was the Cambridge Camden Society, founded in 1839 by an enthusiastic and pugnacious group of young clergy and university students. Their mission was carried forward by expanding membership beyond the university, by circulating masses of cheap and dogmatic pamphlets to the parishes and by publishing a magazine, *The Ecclesiologist* (hence their other name, the Ecclesiologists). No more restrained by fair-mindedness or balance than Pugin's writings, *The Ecclesiologist* made enemies as well as converts by its sarcastic dismissal of anything that strayed from the society's ideals. These included returning medieval churches to a scholarly interpretation of their original form, often at the expense of later, less highly regarded work, the accurate imitation of the most favoured medieval churches in new buildings (a convincingly long chancel for the altar was a particular shibboleth) and a generally 'High' approach to liturgy and theology. But one did not have to swallow the Cambridge gospel whole in order to feel its influence, and the society's assumption of infallibility was often persuasive at a time when architects, clergy and secular patrons were seeking guidance on medieval questions. And so the Gothic Revival grew from a matter of taste or decorum into a disciplined crusade. Henceforth its best buildings were meant to stand apart from what *The Ecclesiologist* called 'the grovelling mass of pagan structures'.

As for Scott, his early enthusiasm for sketching and study had at least supplied an understanding of medieval detail and a repertoire of examples for imitation. Accurately rendered features such as lancet windows therefore appear on his first churches, designed in the late 1830s. However, their plans (with broad lateral transepts instead of a long eastern chancel) were 'modern', as were such features as plaster ornament imitating carved work and un-medieval galleries on cast-iron columns. The new orthodoxy of archaeological fidelity and truthfulness to materials therefore struck Scott like a hammer-blow. The *Recollections* trace this impact back to Pugin and to Cambridge, and especially to the former. The occasion was a nocturnal railway journey in 1840, the source a magazine article by Pugin, later reworked as part of the *True Principles*. Scott felt himself 'from that moment a new man', rescued from 'the abyss into which I had fallen'. And so 'What had for fifteen years been a labour of love only, now became the one business, the one aim, the one overmastering object of my life.'

The echoes in these passages are clear: Scott underwent a secular version of the Evangelical 'conversion experience', a familiar phenomenon within his churchy family circle. This inherited religious background is doubly important, for it gave Scott an inclusive and flexible attitude to liturgy, church planning and Protestant churches abroad. This consorted well with the moderate mainstream of the Church of England, though it would earn him censure from the narrower-minded

High-Church axis at Cambridge. But all this lay in the future; first, Scott rushed to join the medievalists' vanguard, sending off a lengthy apologia-cum-disclaimer for his early churches to the Cambridge Camden Society on New Year's Eve 1841 and signing up as a member himself five weeks later. He also amended the plans for his St Giles, Camberwell, in south London, lengthening its chancel and purging it of 'the viciousness of shams' – the now abhorred plasterwork in imitation of carving. The finished steeple is pyramidal, of the admired English form known as a 'broach type': an aspiring, heaven-soaring design. Inside, the roof follows the medieval practice of exposing and ornamenting the timbers, where a less advanced architect would have supplied a plaster simulation of stone vaulting. (This was the church Scott described in the *Recollections* as the best yet erected.) Another successful competition entry brought him the Martyrs' Memorial in Oxford, modelled on the so-called Eleanor Crosses erected in the 1290s along the funeral route of Edward I's queen. A well-placed calling-card, it led to the no less scholarly restoration and enlargement of the parish church alongside (Scott cited five sources for the new tracery alone). This was the harbinger of his vast future practice reconstructing older churches and cathedrals, sometimes chiefly to save them from collapse, more often to translate them back to an idealised medieval form, and always to make them suitable to developing Victorian ideas of seemly worship.

At this point in the revival it was considered sufficient that a church should look as much as possible like an admired medieval English prototype. Partly as a result, many of Scott's 1840s churches have an impersonal quality and do little to acknowledge regional traditions. The stonespired parish church beside the tracks in Brunel's new railway town at Swindon is an early example. Many architects remained content to take things no further, so that near-replicas of admired thirteenth- and fourteenth-century English churches continued to appear for decades throughout the Anglophone world. But bolder spirits could not rest there, for the great claims made on behalf of Gothic had disruptive, even subversive implications. If the style was indeed morally correct by virtue of truth to materials and construction, what was to prevent imitation of the best Continental examples too? If truth to construction was the watchword, what to do about designing in brick, or the newly cheap, versatile and abundant material of iron? And if Gothic was a universally valid style, what form should new *secular* buildings take?

A MODERN GOTHIC BUILDING

The hotel at St Pancras embodies the new directions taken by the Gothic Revival after 1850. The most iconoclastic buildings of that time were designed by other men, notably the monastically austere High Churchman William Butterfield and Scott's former pupil George Edmund Street. But Scott was never far behind, and in the public mind he soon became identified as the leading figure of the Gothic party. His own thoughts on the future course of the revival are summarised in his book *Remarks on Secular and Domestic Architecture* (1857). By that time Scott was in his creative maturity, so the book provides a context for the design of St Pancras a decade later. This is especially helpful given that Scott failed to leave any definitive account of our building.

First of all, the models for St Pancras are no longer home-grown. Neither is there a single Continental source or period from which its form and motifs derive: this is no exercise in archaeological accuracy, like Scott's churches of the 1840s. The outline owes much to the great town halls and cloth halls of the Low Countries such as Ypres or Brussels, with their high square towers and tiers of pointed windows. But most of the details in London are earlier, deriving in particular from thirteenth-century England or France: simple tracery, projecting oriel windows of stone and sprig-like capitals to the columns. For the materials northern Italy is the chief model: pale stone blocks alternating with red brick around the arches, shafts of polished stone framing the openings below them (for which native granite, as recommended in the *Remarks*, stands in for Italian coloured marble). These details are offset against warm, even walls of undifferentiated red brick: a more restful treatment than the black-chequered work of late medieval England, as seen at Eton College and Hampton Court, or the striated brickwork habitually deployed – often to jolting effect – by Butterfield and Street.

But before this fusion of countries and centuries could be achieved in England, the patriotic blinkers that had been guiding the Gothic Revival had to be cast aside. The surprise is that this should have happened so quickly. A realisation that churches abroad could provide useful models for planning modern ones certainly helped, as did the growing contacts between English medievalists and fellow spirits across the Channel. Scott played his part in fostering these by winning the international competition to rebuild Hamburg's huge Nikolaikirche, destroyed in the city fire of 1842. By way of preparation he mastered German Gothic during a sketching tour of its major sites, conducted with his usual sturdy energy (relieved, if that is the word, by conversations with the pessimist philosopher Schopenhauer, who took his meals in the same Frankfurt hotel in which the architect liked to stay). Regular return trips to oversee construction of the prodigious new church helped to deepen Scott's knowledge of Continental Gothic, even if his home style stayed faithful to English models for some years longer.

The decisive change for Scott happened not long after another Continental tour, in 1851, with the north Italian cities as its chief goal. In Venice 'a most delightful evening' was spent with the critic John Ruskin, whose influential *Seven Lamps of Architecture* (1849) had just proclaimed the intrinsic moral power of Gothic regardless of national school or Roman Catholic origin. For Ruskin, Gothic was 'good' not so much by virtue of structural truth but because its free incorporation of figurative ornament allowed buildings to illustrate and celebrate the natural world, the very work of God. By contrast, the formalised, mass-produced details of classical architecture were at best meaningless, at worst lies derived from pagan temples whose cults were at once false and extinct. Ruskin was also enchanted by the combination of different materials in Italian Gothic, 'structural polychromy', which brought colour and pattern to architecture without compromising Puginian ideals of truth to appearances. He dared to point out, too, how weedy much of England's medieval architecture appeared by the standards of other countries, though he did allow that thirteenth-century English work had potential for development, especially if enriched by decorative motifs from France. These arguments were set out in prose that rises to an astonishing suppleness and beauty, returning again and again to the themes of nature, art and creativity – powers that 'lifted, out of the populous city, grey cliffs of lonely stone, into the midst of sailing birds and silent air'.

It would be a mistake to trace the agenda for High Victorian Gothic back to Ruskin alone. Structural polychromy was a pan-European phenomenon, isolated examples of which appear in England well before 1850; besides, some of its later showpieces – such as Butterfield's huge and stridently patterned Keble College in Oxford – made Ruskin himself blanch. Nor did Ruskin consistently uphold Gothic as the only legitimate style, especially in his later writings and *obiter dicta*. None the less, Scott's later work often shows a decidedly Ruskinian turn, seen for instance in the beautifully aspiring Anglo-French chapel he designed for Exeter College in the same city in 1856. His longstanding interest in carving also fell readily into step with Ruskin's prescriptions, even if the summons back to observation from nature caused him some quandaries. The particular problem here was that some of the most admired medieval carvings seemed not to represent living plants at all. A much-quoted passage in Scott's *Recollections* tells ruefully how he ransacked the botany of England for the original of this mid-thirteenth-century 'stiff-leaf' type but could turn up nothing more plausible than a tiny wall-fern and some varieties of parsley. Even his sleeping hours were invaded: dreaming that he had found the growing plant at last, Scott awoke 'maddened with excitement and pleasure'.

The *Recollections* also admit that Scott's enormous oeuvre had generated 'a vast deal of bad carving … some of it detestable'. But when he kept a close watch the results could be splendid, as the Albert Memorial and St Pancras both show. At the station the carved work includes varieties of foliage and medieval heads on the exterior and an internal population of birds, beasts and flowers, including wiry dragon reliefs set back-to-back over corridor entrances. Much of this is considerably more stylised than would have been the case in the 1850s, when greater naturalism prevailed. Exceptions include four capitals in the booking hall lovingly carved with modern railwaymen at their different tasks, as if to comply with Ruskin's insistence that a building should speak the truth about itself.

There is truthfulness, too, in the way the structure is expressed. 'Shams' such as stucco imitations of carved stone are nowhere to be seen. The different stones employed – red and grey granite, red Mansfield sandstone, and white Ancaster and Ketton stones from the English midlands – stand out against the brickwork, and from each other. Even in the most richly carved blocks, their forms are weighty and solid. There is also a considerable amount of iron on display, in balcony railings and rooftop finials, in such features as the enclosed bridges that carry the first-floor hotel corridor across the two entrance arches, and inside in the boldly exposed girders of the staircase. Contemporaries who considered the Gothic Revival regressive liked to point out that structural ironwork had no part in medieval building, but St Pancras demonstrates the riposte of advanced Gothicists, that the revival was strong enough to assimilate – even to celebrate – the new material, however much it appears here in a secondary role. More than anything else, it is this insistence on the materiality of its own making that marks St Pancras as a child of the Gothic Revival at its creative zenith. Even as it fuses motifs and memories from the past, the building revels in its own

10. A medieval-style capital from the booking hall at St Pancras: a microcosm of the mid-Victorian attempt to infuse modernity with the Age of Faith. The uniformed railwayman is shown applying a brake to a locomotive wheel. Other carvings represent a guard (with a railway carriage), an engine driver and a signal boy.

modernity. An aphorism of another of Scott's great contemporaries, the novelist W. M. Thackeray, seems apt: 'we are of the time of chivalry, and we are of the age of steam.'

Such issues were important, for the Gothic party aimed at nothing less than hegemony over architectural design. For Scott the revival was 'not a mere *fashion*, – it is no *popular caprice*; it is a deep-seated, earnest, and energetic revolution in the human mind'. Thus his *Remarks* volume of 1857, the bland title of which camouflages the non-negotiable demand that public buildings and houses should now be Gothic too. Pugin had urged the same case, but moralistically and excitably; Scott gave more weight to practical counter-arguments in the so-called 'Battle of the Styles', and his book is the stronger for it. His modern Gothic is 'a style which will be pre-eminently that of our own age, and will naturally, readily, and with right good will and heartiness, meet all its requirements, and embrace all its arts, improvements, and inventions'. It is also in a general sense a national style, because it derives from native architectural tradition rather than the revived forms of pagan Antiquity. But in order to reach fulfilment its every element must be re-thought according to contemporary need. If Gothic windows are accused by detractors of being small and gloomy, let them be enlarged, using square-headed forms and sashed glazing when required. Domestic windows should be filled with plate glass, 'one of the most useful and beautiful inventions of our day', reserving patterned glazing for windows with less attractive views – the exact arrangement at St Pancras, where plate glass gives way to patterned for the staircase windows facing Midland Road. The masses of chimneys required for modern living can be turned to advantage by novel grouping and detailing.

As for the steep roofs and gable-ends of Gothic, these are an asset to the designer of house fronts, since they break up the monotonous horizontals of modern city streets. As for the discordant effect of a Gothic public building in such a setting, let it be 'on so vast a scale as to rule its neighbourhood, instead of being governed by it'.

The last fits St Pancras to perfection, but Scott had come close to achieving such a building even earlier, in the shape of the Foreign Office in Whitehall. After some string-pulling he won the competition for this immense and prestigious job in 1858. However, the eclectic modern-Gothic vocabulary of his design proved unacceptable to the new administration headed by Lord Palmerston, which came into office the following year. A very public and increasingly nightmarish two-year tussle followed, as Palmerston refused to accept anything neo-medieval and Scott declined to concede his victory. Prime Ministers being more powerful than architects, the champion of Neo-Gothic kept the commission only because he decided to 'swallow the bitter pill' and swot up the long-unfamiliar forms of classical architecture after all. The resulting Italian Renaissance design, with a few further modifications, is the building that stands today.

What should have been Scott's great leap forward into public secular architecture therefore ended as the most painful episode of his career – so much so that he had to spend two months by the seaside at Scarborough to get over it. That he did not simply resign may have owed something to a wider run of bad luck, his competition entries for town halls at Bradford, Halifax and Hamburg all having recently come to nothing. Even so, his practice in other areas was busier than ever, and it is tempting instead to attribute Scott's tenacity to the deep-seated insecurities, 'unceasing labour and continual worry', that shadow the pages of the *Recollections*. These present his clinging-on as both a matter of principle and a defence of 'a sort of property which Providence had placed in the hands of my family'. His tortured self-justification ('even Mr Ruskin told me that I had done quite right') is embarrassing to read, for Scott plainly understood that his hunger for work had damaged his reputation here, creating the false impression that he was an unprincipled man rather than merely a stubborn one.

After the rise of Modernism forced all historical styles out of fashion, the episode also became notorious as an instance of architecture-as-dressing-up. A thumbnail sketch of it opens Nikolaus Pevsner's *Pioneers of Modern Design* (1960), to demonstrate what the author considered the endemic nineteenth-century sickness, 'the complete lack of feeling for the essential unity of architecture'. A persistent legend even has it that Scott simply recycled his rejected Foreign Office design, cynically or thriftily, as his entry for the competition to build the new hotel up the road at St Pancras.

The truth on the last point is very different. As we have seen, Scott's secular Gothic was meant to be flexible and versatile as well as erudite: a go-anywhere style for the modern age. Well before St Pancras was designed he had already used it for country houses, and for the new town hall at Preston. Scott also tells us that he fought shy of entering the St Pancras competition until prevailed upon by his 'excellent friend' Joseph Lewis, a Midland Railway director. The design was made during another family sojourn at the seaside, this time at Hayling Island, where Scott was detained in the autumn of 1865 by the serious illness of one of his sons.

Railway architecture was a new departure for Scott, and his memoirs note with satisfaction how the project allowed him to adorn London with something in the style of his lamented Foreign Office entry. It has even been suggested that this was his main motivation for entering, which may be mere wisdom after the event: competitions for railway buildings were uncommon, and Scott could have known neither that he would win nor that his later entries to big London competitions would fail.

By means of secular designs of this kind, whether or not they had a life beyond the drawing board, Scott set forth models for a contemporary Gothic style that could be understood, imitated or developed by others. In his own rather mixed metaphor, the Foreign Office style was 'the nucleus on which much which has since been carried out has been founded ... it has often been barbarized into something very execrable, but it has also been the foundation of much that is fairly good'. The results can be seen throughout Britain in the works of dozens of pupils and followers, and Scott even grumbled that his essays in the style were sometimes mistaken for imitations of his own copyists. These circles of influence radiated beyond Britain too: echoes of St Pancras are detectable at what is commonly regarded as the Empire's greatest railway station, the Victoria Terminus ('VT') at Bombay, by F. W. Stevens, completed as late as 1887.

But the final vindication of the Midland Grand Hotel must be its success in formal and functional terms. Viewed from either direction, the clock tower is counterbalanced by the great quadrant sweeping round to the hotel entrance at the opposite end, with its twin spires framing a specially elaborate gable. The intermediate tower over the entrance

Victoria Terminus G. J. P. Ry., Bombay.

11. The magnificent railway terminus at Bombay, commercial capital of the Raj, depicted on a postcard of *c*. 1905. Mughal motifs such as the pointed domes show further development of Scott's prescription for an eclectic modern Gothic style. The red brick walls and stone detailing are familiar from St Pancras; the strict symmetry is not.

roadway gives further visual anchorage to the main front (besides housing an essential facility, the water tank). Gables, oriel windows and other incidents break up the many-windowed ranges between, in just the right measure to prevent monotony. Their placing is slightly irregular, depending on internal convenience rather than the dictates of external symmetry on the Renaissance model. Their size, shape and richness also vary according to the importance of the rooms within; for instance, the bay windows light the sitting-rooms of the biggest suites on each upper floor. It was an article of faith of the Gothicists that progress in architecture depended on this kind of freedom of functional expression. Likewise, the external cab ramp which rises to concourse level is folded comfortably and asymmetrically into the angle made by the western quadrant. The assurance of Scott's composition is doubly remarkable in that neither the quadrant nor the placing of the entrance arches was his invention: both originated in W. H. Barlow's outline plan for the site, in which the arrival and departure routes for passengers and road vehicles were already worked out. So Scott's approach to design was agile and intelligent enough to turn these fixed points to advantage, rather as a landscape gardener will use existing contours and outcrops to best advantage. Those with no time for the Gothic Revival have seen only looseness, swank and clutter in all this; to others the reconciliation of art, function and materials at St Pancras make it a masterpiece.

FORWARD FROM GOTHIC

In visual terms the Midland Grand Hotel is undoubtedly a successful building. However, its designer knew the world too well to believe that architectural development would ever stand still. In the *Remarks* he presented the Gothic Revival in terms of becoming, not being: that is to say, recent efforts in the style, his own included, should be understood as stepping-stones to a comprehensively realised modern style, in which would be united 'the *best ideas* of all other periods and countries'. Mere replication was to be shunned: 'I am no medievalist; I do not advocate the styles of the middle ages as such.' The newly fashionable Italian Gothic buildings should therefore be quarried for motifs and ideas rather than literally replicated, as a few English architects went on to do. His final line urged architects to communal endeavour, in language as muscular as the emerging High Victorian Gothic itself: 'we must unite, one and all, in one steady, unflinching effort, constant, untiring, and in the same direction.' Scott believed, too, that this progress towards the old-new style of the future was directed by 'special interposition of Providence'.

In the first half of the 1870s, when great public buildings such as St Pancras or G. E. Street's new Royal Courts of Justice in the Strand were rising in central London, it was still possible to believe that God's plan for architecture might look something like this. Similar hopes suffuse the closing pages of Charles Locke Eastlake's pioneer history of the revival, published in 1872, which looks forward to a national Gothic school purged of antiquarian literalism and vulgar display. But within another decade the picture looked rather different. Scott and Street were dead, both working to the last, and the coming men of the profession, such as Norman Shaw, T. G. Jackson, J. J. Stevenson, and Scott's own son George Gilbert junior – the last three of whom had been among Scott's pupils – were busy forging a new style.

Measured by strict Renaissance standards, its freedom of planning, composition and expression was medieval enough, but its vocabulary derived from the brick-built classicism of seventeenth-century England. The textures and outlines of this new architecture were commonly gentler, just as its connotations were less churchy and its mood more 'artistic' and feminine – as suggested by its usual (and chronologically rather misleading) label of 'Queen Anne'. It was also less eclectic and cosmopolitan than the modern Gothic represented by St Pancras, though by the 1880s motifs from Renaissance Flanders, Germany and elsewhere were being stirred into the mixture.

Thus was born the characteristic architectural manner of late Victorian England, suitable for a more secular, less patriarchal and hierarchical society. The idea of a universal Gothic style withered; any young architect who chose it as his specialism effectively limited himself to a career centred on the design of churches. For there was an obvious flaw in the dogma that the style of the future should have its roots in the Middle Ages: if the age of Gothic taught freedom of planning and functional expression, and if its motifs could be shuffled and modified to suit modern purposes, why should the same lessons and techniques not be used to rejuvenate other styles? Nor had the Gothicists ever been alone in trying to map out the future of architecture. Two British examples can suffice: a history of architecture by the Regency connoisseur Thomas Hope, published back in 1835, which proposed a kind of fusion-cuisine mixing ideas from every style and school; and the modernised Grecian architecture of straight lintels and reposeful uprights cried up by the Glasgow architect Alexander 'Greek' Thomson, who was stung by his city's decision in 1866 to commission a Sassenach – who else but Scott? – to design its new university, another St Pancras-Gothic edifice. The keenest minds of other countries had been busy with the problem too. As in Britain, they stripped down architecture to its structural constituents, argued variously for round-arched Romanesque, Gothic or Renaissance as the best expression of function and purpose, and puzzled over the proper use and influence of the new materials of iron and glass. The buildings that resulted often fell short of the theoretical originality, at least by the exacting standards of the English Gothic Revival, but the dilemma of style itself was widely understood.

Partisans of classicism were something Scott could cope with, but he was bewildered by the defection of so many young associates to the Queen Anne style, which he called 'a vexatious disturber of the Gothic movement'. Its resurrection of inconvenient Olde Worlde features such as casement windows with leaded lights also ran counter to his sincere faith in progress and modernity. It would doubtless have vexed him even more had he lived to watch the future course of the new secular school of design. Queen Anne houses of the 1870s were not literal re-creations of seventeenth-century models, any more than the new-built 'castles' and 'abbeys' of the Georgians were of medieval ones. Over the next decades, however, architects looked more closely at the 'English Renaissance', and more kindly on its formal and symmetrical aspects. By the 1910s and 1920s many of the smartest new houses in England were almost exact reproductions of Georgian designs, except of course in services and technology. The trajectory is strikingly like that of the Gothic Revival from the eighteenth century to the archaeologically obsessed

1840s. Once more, the quest for progress in architecture only took it back to the past.

This was one way forward from Gothic. Another was to hold hard to the insistence on truth to materials and making: one of Pugin's themes, which became even more dominantly one of Ruskin's. Why did modern manufactures seem so lifeless alongside medieval objects? Part of the answer, Ruskin suggested, was the degraded condition of the modern wage-labourer, denied creative freedom by the iron laws of capitalist production. In a famous passage in *The Seven Lamps of Architecture* he demanded that we ask of any hand-made thing: 'Was it done with any enjoyment – was the carver happy while he was about it?' For Ruskin the disease could not finally be addressed without reforming the society of his own time, in which men were treated 'like fuel to feed the factory smoke'. This greater mission would preoccupy him for the rest of his working life. Some younger talents of the 1850s, including Street's pupils William Morris and Philip Webb, inherited this sense that the paramount question was the way in which things were made, whether buildings or buttons. Issues of mere style had to take second place.

When Webb designed a house for Morris and his wife in 1859, Gothic precedent therefore gave way to a kind of eclectic pragmatism. Sash windows and casements, pointed arches and flattened Georgian-type lintels punctuate its simple red brick walls, which are composed more as an accumulation of volumes than as a series of façades. Its specially made fittings and furnishings anticipated the output of the manufacturing company that Morris and his friends and fellow artists set up in 1861, of which the wallpapers and fabric designs are the most celebrated. It is difficult to decide how far, if at all, the label Neo-Gothic should be applied to any of this. Red House, as the Morris home was called, has therefore been accounted the first building of the nascent Arts and Crafts movement, which sought to overcome the estrangement of designer from maker, architect from artist, and – in its more radical forms – of worker from master and of town from country. Its guiding lights were nostalgic and anti-urban, with medieval guild production a constant inspiration, but it was also more inclusive than the Gothic Revival in what it chose to admire from the past. This led inevitably to some strong affinities with the more questing spirits on the Queen Anne side, the very same who dared to admire the honest and well-made simplicities of early Georgian building.

It will be clear by now that the boundaries between these architectural tendencies could never be exactly drawn. Though Scott conceived of the Gothic Revival as a movement, he could hardly have furnished definitive lists of members and non-members; nor did his own stylistic convictions prevent his relapse into classicism at the Foreign Office. A paternalist Tory of the conventional church-and-state kind, Scott sought only to reform architecture, not to overturn the foundations of the society it served. If the Midland Railway raised capital to carry itself to London and sought to build the grandest hotel in the realm to proclaim the fact, it was none of his business to question the hows or the whys. In this sense the Midland Grand can be said to epitomise the failure of the Gothic Revival as an instrument of radical reform, as Pugin and Ruskin had in their different ways envisaged it.

Nor would one guess from some of Ruskin's writings that he had ever been on friendly terms with Scott. Railways in Ruskin's eyes were instruments of the false idols of material

12. The Midland Railway comes to Monsal Dale, Derbyshire, c. 1862. Quite apart from the noisy trains, the raw new embankments and cuttings were a source of distress to those, like Ruskin, who cherished the seclusion of such wild places.

progress, speed and accelerated exchange. They could also be woefully destructive of the natural beauties that he regarded as the true wealth of human existence, as when the ever-busy Midland blasted a new route towards Manchester through the loveliest parts of the Derbyshire Peak District: 'now, every fool in Buxton can be at Bakewell in half an hour, and every fool in Bakewell at Buxton; which you think a lucrative process of exchange, you Fools everywhere!'

Old age did nothing to moderate these feelings: in 1880 Ruskin added a footnote to the opening sentence of his *Seven Lamps of Architecture* ('Architecture is the art which so disposes and adorns the edifices raised by man ... that the sight of them may contribute to his mental health, power and pleasure'), as follows: 'This separates architecture from a wasp's nest, a rat hole and a railway station.'

A further source of anguish was the onward march of church restoration. Ruskin consistently denounced the practice of replacing decayed or damaged medieval work as a falsification of history, without ever truly addressing the practical problems of how to look after these old buildings. The cause was taken up by William Morris, who in 1877 founded the (still flourishing) Society for the Protection of Ancient Buildings after learning of Scott's plans to tackle Tewkesbury Abbey – or, as the founding manifesto would have it, to reduce the building to a 'feeble and lifeless forgery'. By way of response Scott pointed out that he had always advocated the most careful and conservative treatment of ancient monuments, but it was no good: everyone, himself included, knew that too many of his restorations had been broadbrush affairs, as hastily surveyed and designed as they were inadequately supervised. That Scott's church work had also been a major source of patronage for Morris's own stained-glass manufactures can only have added insult to injury. But Morris was no respecter of persons: his young society was soon embroiled with his former master Street over the architect's plans to restore another great abbey church, Southwell Minster in Nottinghamshire. Morris could be a great hater, too; a private letter written a few years later deplored the fate of another church at the hands of Scott, 'the (happily) dead dog'. For the founders of the Arts and Crafts movement did more than carry forward the ideals of the Gothic Revival; they were also in revolt against some of its most deep-rooted practices and assumptions.

The Arts and Crafts men ultimately had more success making beautiful things than they did in transforming the means of production, but their influence on architecture was none the less profound. By 1900 designers such as C. F. A. Voysey and M. H. Baillie Scott (no relation) had developed a kind of styleless idiom of plain walls and well-made detailing, inspired by the vernacular traditions of farmhouses and cottages but inventive and flexible in its planning. On a more modest scale, Arts and Crafts decencies informed many of the hundreds of thousands of local-authority dwellings built between the wars, when a version of municipal socialism became the national policy for housing.

Few people at that time would have thought to trace the lineage of such projects back to the Gothic Revival. The reputation of nineteenth-century Gothic was then at a low ebb: the obsolete imitation of an archaic style. Even in the 1870s some had questioned whether the language of cathedrals and monasteries was suited to a railway terminus at all; the influential *Quarterly Review* asked facetiously whether the Midland Railway's guards should not also be costumed as beefeaters and its stationmasters as Garter Kings-of-arms. Half a century further on, the essential modernity of Neo-Gothic – the way it had interrogated and remade itself as a universal system of design – was no longer fully understood. The great Victorians had become a bit of joke themselves, with their whiskers, piety, moth-eaten dogmas and naïve artistic naturalism. Even P. G. Wodehouse's Bertie Wooster got the drift, remarking somewhere that if he knew one thing about the Victorians, it was that they weren't to be trusted around a pile of bricks and a trowel. Neither (so it was thought) should they have been let loose near medieval buildings, for a version of Ruskin and Morris's simplistic view that the great restoration campaign had been a Bad Thing had become general currency. When admiration was expressed for Victorian structures, the usual beneficiaries were innovative and visually powerful works of engineering such as bridges or iron-and-glass train sheds. By these lights the true hero at St Pancras was not the architect but the engineer.

3

THE TRAIN SHED

Conceptually as well as physically, there are two ways into St Pancras station. So far we have come in through the hotel, whose design can be fully appreciated only in terms of the Gothic Revival, with all its historical and cultural baggage. The alternative approach is through the train shed, a type of structure no older than the railways themselves, and therefore less weighted with associations. The hotel stirs far-flung memories of Bruges, Salisbury, Caernarfon, Amiens, Verona; by contrast, several of the train shed's most important predecessors stand, or stood, just a short walk away. A few comparisons with these forerunners will show the speedy development of the type, from early makeshifts to the astonishingly achieved and perfected structure that partners Scott's hotel. A comparative tour will also bring out the evolving and often ambiguous relationship between these aggressively novel structures and the frontage buildings which proclaimed the shattering arrival of the railways in the public space of towns and cities.

SOME LONDON PIONEERS

Our first stop is Euston, about a third of a mile west of St Pancras along the Euston Road. The world's earliest long-distance railway, the London and Birmingham, began operating from here in 1837. Viaducts, tunnels and embankments on the line mostly derived from well-tried models developed on the canal system, but the termini were a different matter, for no one was quite sure yet what form this new facility should take. In the event, almost nothing at Euston set an enduring example.

Euston's most famous component, needlessly destroyed when the station was rebuilt in the 1960s and lamented ever since, was a piece of pomp: a titanic free-standing portico in the most austere Greek Doric style, set between pairs of blockish lodges. The first platforms extended perpendicularly behind, where space was also left for the Great Western Railway (which in the event decided not to come this far east). For the first seven years cables worked by stationary engines drew the trains up the incline leading away from these platforms, which was too steep for the early locomotives to climb. In 1838–9 a hotel was added to the buildings, the first erected by any railway company. More strictly, the first two: for twin blocks were provided – linked only by tunnel, and run briefly and incredibly as commercial rivals by separate lessees – in order to preserve a symmetrical and unobstructed view of the entrance. This less than convenient arrangement lasted until the 1880s, when a linking cross-wing hid the 1830s portal after all. In the late 1840s a multi-purpose addition that included a grand hall or passenger concourse was shoehorned in, set to one side. And so the process of piecemeal growth went on.

Euston's train shed was relatively low and was covered by parallel pitched-roofed spans of 'ridge-and-furrow' type made of wrought iron and glass. The brainchild of the engineer Sir Charles Fox, this was essentially a lightweight translation of a timber-framed system developed for greenhouses, such as those created at Chatsworth in Derbyshire by the Duke of Devonshire's head gardener, Joseph Paxton (also a Midland Railway director, wearing another of his hats). The two men collaborated soon after at Paxton's revolutionary Crystal Palace, the apotheosis of the iron ridge-and-furrow technique, built for the Great Exhibition of 1851 with Fox's company as contractor. At Euston extra spans of similar design multiplied as the platforms proliferated. Finally, in 1935 – the same year that it demoted the Midland Grand to office use – the London, Midland and Scottish Railway announced plans to rebuild the formless Euston monster. Delayed by war, work did not begin for a quarter of a century, with results that are as functionally efficient as they are architecturally bland.

Train sheds such as that at Euston were the prevailing type at larger stations during the 1840s, of which the best remaining group can be seen in Dublin. Though readily extendable, their numerous uprights hindered flexible use of space, and their limited height coped poorly with the smoke and steam generated by increasingly frequent and powerful trains (Euston's had to be jacked up by 6 feet in the 1870s). The cast-iron columns supporting the spans were also prone to fracture and collapse if struck by a derailed engine, as happened in London at least once. Wider and higher enclosures were clearly required. The French chose to expand the basic ridge-and-furrow principle, but Britain followed the frequently more spectacular road of giant arched roofs, of which St Pancras is the culmination.

Among the earliest survivors of these arched train sheds

13. Euston Station in a view of 1837, showing the parallel ridge-and-furrow system used for the train shed. At this early date departures were still cable-hauled up the incline beyond the platforms. The diminutive four-wheel carriage in the foreground and the open-topped passenger trucks behind it are both typical of the pioneer years of train travel.

is the Great Northern Railway's terminus at King's Cross, opened in 1852 just east of the future site of St Pancras. Unlike Euston, where architects designed the conspicuously 'architectural' parts and engineers took care of the rest, King's Cross was designed by one man, the architect Lewis Cubitt. Its trains run into twin sheds, each spanning 105 feet (32 metres), with roofs of glass and arched ribs. These were originally of laminated timber, a more economical but less durable material than wrought iron. Given that iron had just been used for the much wider-arched roof at Liverpool's Lime Street station, this was something of a throwback (indeed, Cubitt's timber failed within a few decades, and the present iron ribs replaced them). Laminated arches had precedents in conservatory buildings and at the Royal Navy's naval slipway shelters, but King's Cross looks most unlike either type. Its outer walls are of severely plain brick, broken at the Euston Road end by two huge glazed openings that follow the curves of the train-shed arches. On either side of these openings is a large pier, and a third pier is set between them, in line with the spine wall that separates the train sheds. A much smaller arch, to the right, serves an enclosed cab driveway – later surmounted by extra office storeys – that runs alongside the main enclosure.

The result is a supremely legible building, each part declaring its purpose and means of construction. But one can read such structures for absences as well as presences. At King's Cross the key omission was a station hotel, a facility of some prestige and an irresistible source of potential profit. There was no easy means of tacking one on to a building as tightly organised as Cubitt's. The new Great Northern Hotel – London's second terminus hotel, after that at Euston

14. King's Cross Station, not long after its completion in 1852. The screen wall displays the internal plan with its twin train sheds, between the carriage arch (right) and office wing (left). The Great Northern Hotel appears behind the latter, shown with artistic licence as somewhat richer than the executed building, and to a different, non-curving plan.

– was therefore built on a shallow curving site a little to the west, with its back towards where St Pancras would later rise. It opened two years after the parent station, to designs by the same architect. The façade is a flat affair, with channelled vertical strips at each end and thin classical surrounds to most of the windows: a poor performance judged even against the monster terraces then being built for the denizens of Belgravia or Kensington, let alone against the delirious heights of the future Midland Grand next door.

This hotel was visibly an afterthought. Less apparent are the makeshifts adopted at King's Cross to fit it for efficient operation. The original layout followed early railway practice in providing just two platforms – one for departures, the other for arrivals (hence the twin train sheds) – the rest being given over to carriage sidings. Extra platforms for suburban services were added along the west side of the train shed in the 1870s, just beyond the optimistic little garden provided for the Great Northern Hotel's residents, and in the 1890s some of the sidings inside gave way to new main-line platforms. Various unworthy structures were also added across the front, culminating in a large concourse of the 1970s, which supplements the inconveniently narrow walkway across the inner end of Cubitt's train sheds. In other words, the station has survived in use only because there was space to expand both inside and alongside.

To see a more fully integrated station hotel – the third in the London sequence – we must head westward for two and a half miles to Paddington, where the Great Western Railway opted in the end to build its terminus. In its second incarnation of 1852–4 this has also survived in close to original form. The hotel is placed across the short end of the train shed, where it doubles as the public face of the station, the working areas of which are sunk below ground level. The train shed is entirely iron-framed and subdivided into three parallel enclosures, of which the widest spans 102½ feet (31.25 metres). Unlike at King's Cross, with its weighty spine wall, the divisions between the enclosures are made by airy colonnades. Another difference is the divided responsibility for design: for the Great Western Hotel an outside architect; for the train shed, the Great Western's own engineer, Isambard Kingdom Brunel, in collaboration with the contractors (Sir Charles Fox's firm again), with decorative elements conceived by another architect, Matthew Digby Wyatt. The hotel's Louis XIV interiors were also much more chic than the rooms at the Great Northern Hotel. What the stations have in common is the way they accommodated increasing traffic, for Paddington also fitted in extra platforms and built still more alongside, in this instance adding a neatly matching fourth span to the train shed in Edwardian times.

The lessons for St Pancras seem clear. A train shed should be wide enough for numerous tracks and platforms, with plenty of space overhead. It should also be planned in a close relationship to the station hotel, and to the other working parts of the terminus. Paddington fits these criteria, as did two less well-preserved London termini built for the South Eastern Railway a decade or so afterwards: Charing Cross, with a train shed 164 feet (50 metres) wide, and Cannon Street, where the span measured 190 feet (58 metres). The chief difference at St Pancras is the sheer scale, especially of the train shed, which at 245½ feet (74.8 metres) was the widest single-span structure the world had yet seen. This was enough to straddle five platforms, later increased by infilling of sidings to seven. Scott had no part in its design, or in determining its relationship to the proposed hotel and station offices. Both tasks were undertaken by the Midland Railway's consulting engineer, William Henry Barlow.

BARLOW SOLVES THE PROBLEM

Barlow's train shed was conceived and built within a discipline very different from that of the Victorian architect. For Scott the highest endeavour was the adaptation and development of historical styles within the limitations supplied by the client. For the engineer a problem may be stated simply, then solved step by step within the technology and budget available. All being well, aesthetics will take care of themselves – or, put another way, the process may generate its own, functional aesthetic. Which may sound a little too good to be true; and yet at St Pancras we know that this is pretty much how things happened. This is because Barlow left his own account of the project, in the shape of a marvellously lucid paper delivered to the Institution of Civil Engineers in 1870. His design had benefited from discussions with another very able consulting engineer, Rowland Mawson Ordish – the two had collaborated on aspects of the Crystal Palace back in 1851, and later Ordish also advised Scott on iron-framing matters – but there is no reason to divide the credit for the concept or the leading motifs.

Barlow's central problem was this: to supply a sheltered enclosure of the maximum width available from the site, raised nearly 20 feet (6 metres) above the streets around, and leaving space for the hotel at the south end. In addition, he had to adjust his design to allow for the presence of a railway tunnel under the site, and to work out how to treat the enclosed volume under the platforms. The other chief constraint was width, for the site was confined by streets on each side, with no prospect of expansion. Everything flowed from these stipulations.

Before considering the great structure arching above it, the elevated platform deck calls for explanation, given that the height was unhelpful in terms of circulation of passengers and goods. The answer lies some way beyond the station site, in the immovable form of the Regent's Canal, the legacy of a previous cycle of the Industrial Revolution, which the approach tracks had somehow to traverse. Barlow chose to carry his line over the canal by means of a bridge and to continue it into the station by means of a lengthy viaduct. London's railways offered plenty of precedents for the latter, beginning with the London and Greenwich line, opened from London Bridge station in the 1830s. Putting the platforms up in the air in this way had its drawbacks, but at St Pancras the level approach avoided the greater evil of a steep gradient rising immediately outside the station, something that even the most powerful steam locomotives found hard to climb from a standing start. An approach that tunnelled under the canal would also have been possible – that was just what the Great Northern had done to reach King's Cross – but only at much greater expense and disruption. It was bad enough that the company was already being compelled by the authorities to meet the costs of diverting the 'black and foetid torrent' of the Fleet (one of London's ancient rivers, long since overwhelmed by sewage) into a huge new cast-iron conduit under the station, as well as enclosing its course a little way up the line at Kentish Town. The visual lift that the elevated platforms transmitted to the train shed was thus an unsought by-product of the urban context.

Next, how to enclose this elevated deck? Barlow at first considered twin train sheds, after the pattern of King's Cross. But he also appreciated the advantages of a single-span roof in terms of the flexible planning of tracks and platforms – the 'loose-fit' principle, to borrow a late twentieth-century term – even if the span required was so much wider than anything yet built. Barlow was led to take his daring leap by a rather unexpected route, as it were from the bottom up. For the construction site did not just encompass the tracks into the new terminus: there was also to be a railway tunnel beneath the station area, excavated to allow the Midland to join up – via the underground lines of the Metropolitan Railway – with the cross-London route of a southern ally, the London, Chatham and Dover Railway. (All but three hundred of the graves disturbed in St Pancras's churchyard were actually casualties of this tunnel and not of the main line proper.) The tunnel was essential to the finances of the company's London extension project, for it allowed coal to be hauled very profitably from the midlands to the south London suburbs and beyond. None of this would have been apparent to travellers at its showpiece terminus up above, who themselves represented only one of the sources of revenue for which the Midland had come to the capital: a reminder that Victorian railways were the chief carriers of long-distance inland freight as well as people.

Barlow's first intention was that the spoil dug out for the tunnel should be used to infill the basement under his elevated platforms. Wiser counsels then suggested that this space would be better turned over to commerce, especially if this could be tied in with the railway's own goods traffic. As it happened, there was growing demand in London for the fine ales of Burton-upon-Trent in Staffordshire, near the heart of the Midland system. The soft water and improved brewing techniques there allowed the production of a clear and stable brew very different from the capital's darker and cloudier stouts and porters, a change in taste that also contributed to the slow disappearance of pewter tankards from pubs in favour of drinking glasses. The railway had already erected a beer trans-shipment warehouse for Messrs Bass alongside the nearby canal, a structure big enough to provide six acres of storage space: in brewer's terms, enough for 100,000 thirty-six-gallon barrels; in drinker's terms, enough for 28,800,000 pints. The huge void beneath the new station platforms, with its deep plan and stable temperature, was ideal for the same purpose and could easily be reached from track level by means of hydraulic lifts.

In order to exploit the basement space to the maximum, Barlow therefore dispensed with the normal mid-Victorian structural system of brick piers and arches in favour of even ranks of some eight hundred uniform cast-iron columns. These supported a grid of two thousand wrought-iron girders, which in turn underlay the iron plates on which the tracks and platforms rested. The spacing of the columns at centres just over 14 feet apart was calculated to match the plans of the beer warehouses of Burton-upon-Trent, where the same figure derived from a multiple of the standard local cask. And so, in Barlow's words, 'the length of a beer barrel became the unit of measure upon which all the arrangements of this floor were based'. This modular system of design was not new – the Crystal Palace had already demonstrated what

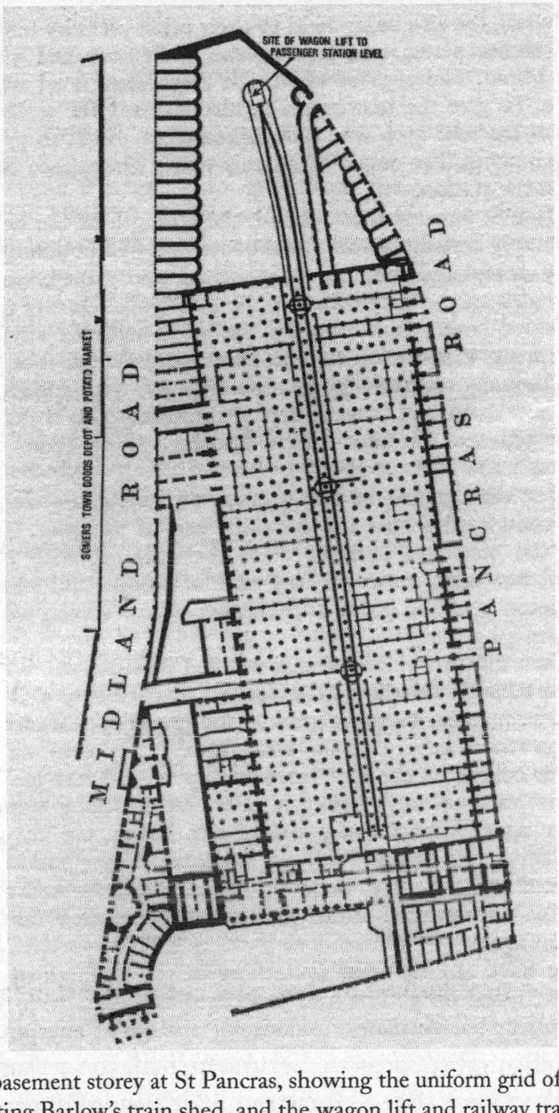
SITE OF WAGON LIFT TO PASSENGER STATION LEVEL
SOMERS TOWN GOODS DEPOT AND POTATO MARKET
MIDLAND ROAD
PANCRAS ROAD

15. The basement storey at St Pancras, showing the uniform grid of columns supporting Barlow's train shed, and the wagon lift and railway tracks that allowed the spaces between to warehouse barrels of beer.

could be achieved by standardized parts on an even structural grid – but it had never before been used to organise the substructure of a railway terminus. Such was the capacity of this new beer cellar that three dedicated trains loaded with casks arrived every day to replenish it, with even more coming in October, the peak month for brewing.

There was no reason why an iron-framed substructure such as this could not have been twinned with a subdivided train shed as at King's Cross, provided that a sufficiently strong spine wall was built to support the central line of roof supports. However, Barlow saw that this would pile an unwelcome extra load on the crown of the brick-vaulted railway tunnel beneath the site, which would therefore need to be expensively reinforced. A spine wall set midway would also have multiplied the number of types of beam needed for the ironwork sections, eroding the expected economies of scale. But if the interlinked girders were allowed instead to run across the entire width of the station without interruption by a wall, they could double as the ties of a single-arched roof, acting like strings across the upward-facing bows formed by the curving ribs. This would effectively create a series of giant trusses – of which the cross-members were buried below the surface – the trains running in and out as it were just above the bowstrings.

It followed that rainwater falling on the roof would all run down the outer sides rather than into a valley between twin roofs, from which it would have to be conveyed down and out through the structure. This, too, was far from negligible as a saving in construction costs. Yet another advantage came with the effective burial of the horizontal girders. Metal constructions are not static: they expand and contract considerably as the temperature rises or falls. Thermal expansion of this kind had to be allowed for with more than ordinary care when a metal structure was housed within a rigid shell of brick, as at St Pancras. But the temperature of the girders under the platforms, shielded alike from sunlight, ice or snow, would always be much more stable. This minimised what Barlow called the 'racking motion' that afflicted other large metal-framed structures, which usually had to be accommodated by means of costly extras such as roller-frames at the feet of the principal uprights. The exposed sections at St Pancras would certainly still expand and contract, but this could be contained within the curve of the arch. And so, Barlow concluded, 'the only effect would be a slight rise or fall in the crown' – like the shallow breathing of a mighty creature in its sleep.

Barlow invoked all these economies to justify his estimate that a giant single-span roof would be markedly cheaper than a lower double one, at £4 rather than £5 per square yard enclosed. It may be that this was wishful thinking, in which case it may also be that the Midland Railway's directors col-luded in it for the sake of company glory. Certainly there is nothing parsimonious-looking about the finished result. Rather, the system of securing the arches out of sight below the platforms gives the structure a power and clarity all its own, since it avoids the need for additional bracing within the curve of the arch. The usual method of providing this in the bigger train sheds that came before St Pancras was by means of crescent- or sickle-trusses: secondary arches of a slightly larger radius sitting within the main arches, and rising to a lower apex. Any tendency of the main arches to flex outwards was contained by the tautening effect of the inner ones, to which they were secured by wrought-iron ties at regular intervals. This was the system used at the London and North Western Railway's pioneering train shed of 1849 at Liverpool Lime Street, already mentioned, which at 153½ feet comfortably took the world record for a single-span structure; yet it was surpassed just five years later by the same company's 212-foot prodigy at Birmingham New Street, a domestic record that would stand until St Pancras was built. The most ambitious of London's other termini of the 1860s, Charing Cross and Cannon Street, also had roofs of sickle-truss type. All these have gone: Charing Cross rebuilt to a different design after a fatal collapse in 1905, when a faulty tie-rod fractured; Cannon Street blasted to an unglazed skeleton during the Blitz and dismantled in the 1950s; Birmingham also an air-raid casualty. However, passengers arriving at Liverpool can still marvel at the replacement train shed of 1867, of the same sickle-truss type, and of a width matching that of the lost pioneer down the line at Birmingham.

Barlow's arches are quite different. Each arm is composed of sturdy parallel members made up of riveted iron plates, conjoined by fifteen main braces and a lattice of fifty cross-braces. Riveted plate construction of this type was relatively cheap and simple, being essentially the same as the usual method for building iron railway bridges. Every arch is linked to its neighbours by means of longitudinal and diagonal braces, which double as the framing for the roof cladding – originally solid below, but with two and a half acres of glazing within the sections closer to the crown. There are twenty-five arches in all, set at intervals of 29 feet 4 inches, double the spacing of the basement columns – the Burtonian beer-barrels' controlling influence again – to form an enclosure 689 feet (210 metres) long. Much of

16. A contrast in train-shed design. Birmingham New Street, above, illustrates the spidery effect of sickle-truss construction. At St Pancras, shown below on a postcard of 1907, the space flows through unobstructed.

the visual power of this huge interior comes from the way in which these soaring arches allow the eye to calibrate the space immediately. Here are none of the distracting webs of sub-arches, braces and rods required by a sickle-truss roof, which tend to coalesce into a kind of visual mist in longer views (Scott called the system 'spider-like'). As if to perfect this sense of volumetric clarity, the ends are closed off by big, simply detailed iron-and-glass screens. The screen at the departure end comes down to some 30 feet above the carriage roofs, appearing from within the station not unlike a transparent theatre curtain frozen short of the stage. Its counterpart at the hotel end owes its existence to Scott, who insisted that the rooms behind it should have protection from the trains' noise and smoke – a blessing omitted at certain other terminus hotels, Charing Cross included.

Nor do the differences from earlier train sheds end here. The more ambitious of these had round-arched roofs, of profiles variously elliptical, segmental or semicircular. But at St Pancras the roof rises in an elegantly graduated profile, terminating in a pronounced point. Frederick Williams's company history of 1876 compared the outline to a pair of lobster's claws, but it is also recognisable to the medievalist's eye as a four-centred arch of late Gothic type. This summit reached higher than a round-topped arch would have done, to a prodigious 105 feet (32 metres) above the level of the rails, which made St Pancras the tallest train shed ever built, as well as the widest. No one had seen anything like this space before, and time has done little to diminish its tremendous impact. A century after its completion the critic Ian Nairn called it 'a vast throbbing hangar; the phrase needs to be repeated sixteen times to make enough weight in the book and convey the overwhelming solid force of this beginning or end to journeys.'

The affinity between the pointed profile and Scott's Neo-Gothic station building has caused some confusion as to whether Barlow intended his roof to carry a medieval echo. Certainly the engineer's own account allowed that the shape contributed to the 'architectural effect', but he explained its true genesis as a way of strengthening the train shed against wind stress. (So stable is the design that the modern-day engineers who adapted it for the Eurostar services have speculated whether the arches might have been able to stand even without the cross-girders across the bottom.) Indeed, the train-shed design was finally endorsed on 3 May 1865, at the same committee meeting that decided to put the hotel design out to competition. Scott's *Recollections* also mention that the pointed arch was a fait accompli when he began. Only in the details can there have been consultation, as contract drawings for the roof were not agreed until July 1866, three months after Scott's designs were accepted in what was meant to be their final form. Barlow's drawings show the distinctive cast-iron openwork traceries in the upper angle between each truss and the outer wall: an infusion of 'style' to help reconcile the train shed's spare lines with its enclosure of brick and stone. Though structurally independent, this enclosure is an essential part of the experience of the train shed, which is effectively bounded on three sides by two inward-facing Neo-Gothic storeys. Once the visitor has absorbed the impact of the roof, these architectural elements come more fully into play, especially for those scanning the space for the refreshment rooms, bookstalls and other facilities that open off the sides. The result is to reinforce the functional relationship between train shed and frontage building, the main entrances and exits of which were determined by Barlow before Scott came on the scene.

The method used to erect the train shed also illustrates to perfection the mixture of past experience, heroic improvisation and raw muscle that created the Victorian railway system. Here the key precedent was the use of movable timber stages or platforms which could traverse the length of the structure as it was erected, a method first applied to train-shed construction at Birmingham New Street. By allowing the iron framework to be assembled in situ, a staging offered clear advantages over the technique used at King's Cross, where the arches were put together flat on the ground and hoisted into position one by one in the venerable tradition of timber-framed barn building. Two huge construction stagings were provided at St Pancras, to a design by the manager of the Butterley Company, the contractors for the ironwork (Barlow insisted on the second one in order to speed up the company's faltering schedule). Each was assembled in three sections and contained fully eight miles of structural timber. When ironwork fixings and load were allowed for, this gave a working weight of 1,300 tons: about thirty-five times that of the larger locomotives of the day. Each section of the scaffoldings likewise moved on wheels running on rails, but they progressed without the aid of steam traction, as described by Frederick Williams:

A workman was stationed at each wheel, who placed a crowbar in such a position that it could be brought to bear against the wheel. When all were ready, a signal-man stood with a loose iron plate and a hammer, which were to serve as a gong, and the

moment he struck it each workman pressed his crowbar lever-
like against the wheel. The whole mass at once moved forward
a distance of about an inch and a half, and this with very little
exertion on the part of the men.

So says the official version; but how many of the men had
Williams tracked down to ask?

Back to the matter of pointed arches. Here it is instructive to compare some later train sheds that adopted the St
Pancras model of very wide lattice-girder spans. Manchester
Central (now the G-MEX exhibition centre) also has arches
anchored in the foundations, but they are of unpointed, segmental profile. Glasgow's St Enoch terminus, demolished
in the 1970s, was similar. But the pointed-arched shape was
repeated too, for instance at the later train sheds at Cologne
and Berlin Friedrichstrasse. America took to the St Pancras
model especially avidly. The 1871 incarnation of New York's
Grand Central, truly the grandest station built in the United
States up to that time, was meant to rival the best that Old
Europe could show. Its paymaster, the railroad baron Cornelius
Vanderbilt, therefore insisted that it be the largest station in
the world: five acres in extent rather than the four and a half
of St Pancras. The train shed adopted Barlow's model of
soaring arches tied below the tracks, but of segmental form.
At Park Square station at Boston (1872) the pointed form
prevailed. Neither was as wide as the St Pancras train shed,
which finally lost its record to the Pennsylvania Railroad's
Jersey City station of 1888, where the span was just ten feet
wider. Within a year the title re-crossed the Atlantic, to the
short-lived Galérie des Machines in Paris, with its staggering
111-metre (364-foot) span. This was another with a pointed

profile, though now of more advanced three-hinged, self-bracing design.

Barlow lived to see this marvel, and beyond: he died in 1902, twenty-four years after Scott, his senior by just one year. Not long after his work at St Pancras was complete, Barlow predicted that any records set by such iron structures would eventually be broken in steel, and much of the later part of his long career was spent on calculating safe stress levels for the use of the newer material. His eminence in many fields was recognised by the French, who made him an honorary member of the Société des Ingénieurs Civils de France. Indeed, Barlow's curriculum vitae is one of achievement, prosperity and acclaim throughout. In his early twenties he oversaw the modernisation of the ordnance and lighthouses at Constantinople, for which the Sultan appointed him to the *Nichan Iftikhar*, or Order of Glory; in his thirty-eighth year he became an exceptionally youthful Fellow of the Royal Society; and so on. But in human terms Barlow now seems remote: he left no memoir and has found no biographer, and even the date of his marriage has not been discovered. Can his inner life have been as troubled and self-reproachful as Scott's? We are unlikely ever to know.

The French and American locations mentioned are reminders that late nineteenth-century Britain was industrial top dog no longer. Further confirmation came in the form of the Eiffel Tower – like the Galérie des Machines, a commission for the Paris Exhibition of 1889 – which carried off the record for the world's tallest building. Neither structure tried to reproduce a past architectural style any more than London's own Crystal Palace had done when it initiated the fashion for international exhibitions back in 1851. As nineteenth-century

17. The 1871 incarnation of New York's Grand Central Station. As at St
Pancras, the skeleton is formed by latticed arches tied invisibly below
platform level. The carriages (right) run on pivoting bogies, an American
improvement introduced to Britain when the ever-enterprising Midland
Railway imported the first Pullman cars in 1874.

architects wrestled over the style of the future, some contemporaries were asking whether the way had not already been shown by such engineering-led structures. St Pancras has often been read as a microcosm of this division: a hotel that looks back unashamedly to feudal times, yoked to a train shed conceived in terms of contemporary needs, a true ancestor of today's giant open-plan warehouses, airliner hangars and super-bowls. As if to underline the point, the simpler, more forthright King's Cross building sits right alongside.

KING'S CROSS AS MODERN MODEL

King's Cross is the most explicitly functional, the least 'styled', of the great London termini. As *The Builder* magazine announced in 1851, its effect depends 'on the largeness of some of the features, its fitness for its purpose and its characteristic expression of that purpose'. The key word is 'effect': plenty of the details go beyond utility, even if they play only secondary roles. The rather puny clock turret on top of the central pier – sometimes called the first station clock, but actually a reprise from Lewis Cubitt's earlier station designs in Surrey and Kent – is treated in the Italianate fashion, with a shallow pyramid roof. Less apparent nowadays is the ornamentally grooved brickwork around the original entrances, now hidden by the 1970s concourse extension. The three-storey offices along the west side, where they balance the cab road, are treated in a spare classical style, including triple windows of the so-called Venetian type. By such small but telling touches Cubitt signalled that his building was to be classed with the more austere kind of architecture rather than as 'pure' engineering.

This plain-speaking was not without admirers even in the mid-Victorian decades, when sheer, simplified architecture such as that of the later Georgians was commonly despised. The same *Quarterly Review* critic who found the rich Gothic frontage of St Pancras 'a complete travesty of noble associations' also praised King's Cross as 'simple, characteristic, and true. No one would mistake its nature and use.' In fact the giant semicircular windows that are its most memorable device were not repeated on this scale at any other British station, unlike on the Continent or across the Atlantic: witness the Gare du Nord in Paris or the rebuilt and explicitly Roman Grand Central in New York. But this singularity doubtless served only to fix King's Cross more firmly in the mind.

Curiously, Scott himself took a position similar to that of the *Quarterly's* in his own *Remarks* of 1857, where he praised the hefty brick-built engine sheds at Camden Town on the approach to Euston as the best kind of utilitarian architecture: 'though what mouldings they have are Roman, their whole aspect is that of Gothic buildings'. By this he meant that structures that showed sufficient truth to materials and function were compatible with the architectural principles set forth by Pugin. Conversely, Scott had little time for the carnival of styles used for railway stations up to that point: 'Some are profusely decorated Elizabethan, some are very bad Gothic; others are in the Italian palatial style; others, again, miserable travesties of the Crystal Palace.' Behind these remarks must lurk some of Pugin's more optimistic pronouncements about the ease with which railway viaducts and stations would translate into medieval architectural language. (Surprisingly, Pugin accepted the railways – and just as well, since his frenzied work-chasing would have been impossible without them). But neither Pugin nor the railway-hating Ruskin could reconcile himself to an architecture of iron and glass, the epitome of rootless, industrialised modernity. Scott at least understood structural iron well enough to use it creatively and efficiently in otherwise traditionally solid-walled buildings, but almost always – in both senses – in a supporting role. And as we have seen, his high hopes that Gothic might generate a new style by a kind of Darwinian struggle foundered when an ungrateful younger generation turned instead to other schools of revivalism.

The failure of nineteenth-century architects to realise a 'style of the future' based more fundamentally on metal and glass was a familiar lament in Modernist architectural writing between the wars. For Modernists, then and now, the essence of truth is the rational and functional use of materials, which are assumed to be standardised and mass-produced. In the words of Mies van der Rohe, 'Only an architecture arrived at by the explicit use of available building materials can be justified in moral terms.' By the inventive and economical solution of problems within these constraints, architects create new forms and types of building. Like Pugin, Modernists were prone to assert that this new architecture embodied principles rather than 'style', a word with connotations of superficiality and self-indulgence; unlike him, they rejected the vocabulary and associations of every phase of the architectural past. The Gothic arch and the Grecian column belonged alike in the dustbin of history.

Modernists of a leftish cast of mind – which in mid-twentieth-century Britain meant the majority – looked beyond these formal and technical imperatives to a planned future in which the new architecture would play its part in satisfying communal human needs. An extreme version of this universal planning was set out in the writings of Le Corbusier, who celebrated the purposeful beauty of motor cars and ocean liners, and whose most famous dictum has passed into the language: that the house is a *machine à habiter*, a machine for living in. Such a harsh and abstract programme was not for everyone, however, and in Britain the new school was soon re-interpreting the native architectural past. In this way, it was hoped, indigenous traditions of building could be foster-parents to the new school of design, which would grow up speaking with a native accent. The Arts and Crafts movement had already shown the way by renouncing 'architecture' for honest, practical 'building', indifferent to the pedantries of historical style. British Modernists found a comparably honest directness in what was soon labelled the 'Functional Tradition', exemplified by plain, clean-lined railway viaducts and sheer-walled mills and warehouses. Similarly, the Regency terraced house was now commended for its compact planning and unadorned façade, rather than for the classically derived proportions admired by the Neo-Georgian party. King's Cross ticked all the boxes too: form follows function inside and out, materials are honestly and enterprisingly used, and the building was both modern in its day and relevant to contemporary needs. A drawing of it even appears, captioned 'The sane architecture of the nineteenth century', in J. M. Richards' Pelican paperback *An Introduction to Modern Architecture* (1940), the first mass-market book on the subject published in Britain. The station's designer is falsely but tellingly identified as an engineer; the adjacent text stresses the need to develop a common architectural language without the crutch of period revival.

And so the two stations, conveniently juxtaposed, and familiar as household words, became stock figures in British architectural writing. By 1953 the scholar-architect Harry Goodhart-Rendel noted that King's Cross 'has been hailed with relief by three generations of critics because of its freedom from irrelevant motifs of applied architecture'. A few generous spirits still admired Scott's building too – the refugee German art historian Nikolaus Pevsner commended its 'bewildering splendour' in 1943 – but a more typical diagnosis was that of Goodhart-Rendel, that it was a failure because 'much too self-consciously stylistic'.

Above all, the way in which Scott's design had been separated from that of Barlow's train shed was a recurrent cause of complaint. In lecture of 1968 to Columbia University Sir John Summerson, the leading British-born architectural historian of Pevsner's generation, bewailed 'the disintegration of architecture and engineering: the total separation of functional and "artistic" criteria, in separate heads and hands', in contrast to the 'acceptable union' of King's Cross. This goes beyond the lament over the 'lack of feeling for the essential unity of architecture' that Pevsner diagnosed in the Foreign Office débâcle, where Scott cast his styles on and off like costume changes: it locates the very essence of Victorian architecture – and, by extension, Victorian society – in self-contradiction. The critic Robert Furneaux Jordan, writing in the popular Thames and Hudson *World of Art* series not long afterwards, chimed in: Scott's hotel is 'the culminating masterpiece of its epoch' only in that 'It combines all the qualities of the [eighteen-] sixties: stylistic display and solid philistinism'. At St Pancras 'There is no evidence that it ever occurred to anyone that a station and a hotel might be designed by one man.' The reason for this malaise: 'The mind of Victorian England was divided between its ideals and its materialism. The attempt to reconcile them – to boss one's factory hands during the day, and to read Tennyson or Carlyle in the evening – has exposed the age to the charge of hypocrisy. This schizophrenia is most marked in architecture.' St Pancras as mental illness: even the *Quarterly Review* had not gone that far. But the lament that a single designer was not employed at St Pancras also brings some very different stations into focus.

4

ENGINEERS' ARCHITECTURE,

ARCHITECTS' ENGINEERING

St Pancras was a latecomer to the ranks of the London termini. By the time it was conceived, the professions of architecture and engineering had grown further apart than in the days when Lewis Cubitt was able to double up in both roles at King's Cross. At Euston the division of labour between architects and engineers contributed to a muddle; at Paddington the professions collaborated with happier results, though without achieving the full integration of train shed and hotel. The conclusion voiced by Furneaux Jordan, that a single designer was best of all, may seem tempting (provided that one allows for some creative interdependence with those unsung heroes the builder/contractors). But a couple of trips outside London will show that things were not quite so simple.

First to Bristol, at the far end of the Great Western's original main line from Paddington. The first station here opened at Temple Meads in 1840 and now survives in museum ownership. Brunel seems to have designed it without co-opting an architect, which means that the building can take its place in his long and astonishingly diverse list of projects: the Clifton Suspension Bridge and Royal Albert Bridge; prefabricated hospitals for the Crimea; the world's first screw-driven vessel, the SS *Great Britain*, and its largest ship to date, the SS *Great Eastern*; the pneumatically powered Atmospheric Railway; the Great Western Railway itself. That some of these schemes were collaborations and others fatally misconceived has detracted little from Brunel's heroic legend, and his remarkable 390,000 votes – second only to Churchill – in a BBC 'Greatest Briton' poll in 2002 suggests a continuing affinity with our own technocratic and entrepreneurial culture.

Brunel's frontage building at Bristol may therefore come as a surprise. Here is no functionalist exercise in the manner of King's Cross, but an unmistakable attempt at early Tudor Gothic, turreted and battlemented, with gatehouse-like features at each end. Stranger still, his train shed is treated in a Gothic manner too. It has aisles formed by arcades of cast-iron columns, the arches of which are shallow-pointed in the late medieval English fashion. Iron-plated timber beams slant up from above these arcades to the apex of the roof, over the tracks. These beams are apparently supported at their lower ends by lesser half-arches, of the hammerbeam type – that is, half-arches attached to upright posts onto which the main span seems to join. Though hopelessly wrong in their proportions, these extra arches and posts are clearly meant to enhance the 'Old English' character of the interior. To the educated early Victorian traveller they would instantly have recalled stately interiors such as Richard II's Westminster Hall or Henry VIII's Hampton Court. But in those buildings the hammerbeam method was used to counter the tendency of a roof with an open central span to force the walls outwards. Brunel's hammerbeams and half-arches were structurally redundant, meant only for show.

18. Bristol Temple Meads Station, where Brunel dressed up his utilitarian timber roof in the forms of late medieval English architecture. The tracks are laid to his ill-fated 'broad gauge', 7 ft ¼ in. apart: an unsuccessful rival to George and Robert Stephenson's standard gauge of 4 ft 8½ in., used elsewhere in Britain and adopted in most of the rest of the world.

By the stern standards of the Functional Tradition, both building and train shed are therefore severely wanting. For Brunel categorically rejected simplicity and austerity at Bristol in favour of a historical style calculated for grandeur and decorum – a late medieval style, in deference to England's greatest medieval city outside London – and he persisted with it even in those parts of his structure that relied most heavily on novel methods and materials. (The implacable Pugin thought Brunel's Great Western Gothic 'at once costly, and offensive, and full of pretension', but then Pugin said that kind of thing all the time.) In short, given a major station all to himself, the great engineer responded just like any style-and-period-fixated Victorian architect.

That these roles could also be reversed is indicated by the central station at Newcastle upon Tyne, begun in 1846 and finished in 1863. Here the frontage is proudly classical, including a mighty stone portico of the drive-through type known as a *porte-cochère*. Behind it is an iron and glass train shed constructed in 1849–50, over 700 feet (213 metres) long, and of extreme lightness and grace. As at many major stations outside London, tracks enter it from both ends, roughly parallel to the frontage building. Like the slightly later example at Paddington, it takes the form of three parallel spans, but here they are laid out on a visually bewitching slow curve with a maximum radius of 800 feet (244 metres). The arches are formed by segmental-arched girders, of a novel and influential type that was achieved by passing the hot iron between bevelled rollers. Apart from a few mouldings on the supporting columns, there is no 'period' detail to place the train shed under the protecting sign of a familiar culture or style.

The station's accredited designer was John Dobson, the

premier architect of the age in north-east England. However, the originality of the train shed led in the twentieth century to suspicions that it was ghosted by a 'proper' engineer, probably the railway specialist Robert Stephenson and his assistant. Not so; for recent research has confirmed that the concept was truly Dobson's own, realised by close collaboration with the ironwork contractors – an extraordinary leap for a man born as far back as 1787, whose first buildings were completed two decades before railway stations as such even existed. So the train shed is a clear case of a Victorian architect acting like an engineer: the mirror-image of Brunel at Bristol.

Furneaux Jordan's comments over St Pancras thus represent a grab at the wrong end of the stick. Dignity and propriety required the external face of a Victorian station to adopt one of the styles considered appropriate to public architecture. This might be applied lightly to the bones of the structure, as at King's Cross, or more lavishly, as at Bristol and Newcastle. An exceptional architect such as Dobson might design the train shed too; an exceptional engineer such as Brunel might also design the 'architectural' frontage building. A station hotel, being both residential and exclusive – a kind of multiple-occupancy mansion – was also expected to speak the language of style. The Midland Railway would no more have made the one at St Pancras as stark as a grain warehouse than it would have embellished a grain warehouse to the point at which it might be mistaken for a hotel. The train shed behind it was a different matter, not just because its structure and materials were outside the frames of reference of the historical styles of architecture, but because it did not have to join in the system of visual transactions by which the Victorian city expressed itself. (Brunel's train shed at Temple

19. The beautiful station at Newcastle upon Tyne, where the arched iron-framed roof was born in 1849–50. The system of parallel spans was taken up at other stations built on a curve, such as York, where a single giant span would not have been practicable.

Meads is the exception proving the rule, for its hammerbeam system failed to set a wider trend.)

On a practical level the division of design was no drawback as long as the two parts functioned well together. Recent re-examination of the sources has shown the care with which this boundary was drawn at St Pancras: Barlow worked out the routes by which road vehicles and passengers would enter and leave the station and shaped the hotel's foundation plan to suit; Scott developed the main emphases of his building around these fixed points and alignments. The different materials and structural systems used by the two men therefore camouflage their deeper interdependence.

Besides, even if the idea of a single designer had prevailed at St Pancras, by the late 1860s there were no longer Brunels or Dobsons available to do the work. Scott and his office no more had the expertise to design a structure as novel and audacious as the St Pancras train shed than Barlow could have come up with a luxurious hotel expressed in advanced and coherent Neo-Gothic. The future belonged to specialisation: a separate Institution of Mechanical Engineers had existed since 1847 (dominated at first, significantly, by locomotive designers); the electrical and telegraph engineers went their own way in 1871, leaving the Institution of Civil Engineers to concentrate on construction. The division of design on the buildings side was never absolute: smaller stations remained part of the railway company engineer's everyday responsibilities well into the twentieth century (sometimes reworking a basic model supplied by an architect), while any architect of ambition needed to keep up with new materials and construction techniques coming from the engineering side. The abandonment of the styles of the past in the twentieth century changed the terms on which architects depended on engineers to make their projects work, but left the creative tension between them unresolved.

PAYING THE HOTEL BILL

Architecture is often discussed in terms of what can be read in the fabric of a building: plan, style, materials. A more searching account may seek to establish the needs a building was intended to satisfy and the problems the architect attempted to solve along the way. Still more intangible in its effects is the route by which a building is commissioned and paid for in the first place: 'procurement', in modern usage. The point may seem banal, but its implications are too easily overlooked. In the case of Victorian railway stations the most important of these is that the companies' directors and managers were ultimately answerable to shareholders wanting the best return on their money.

Viewed in this light, King's Cross suddenly looks rather different. Before construction even started, the Great Northern had to find half a million pounds simply to survey and enact the route of its new main line (the British method of railway building by act of Parliament was a golden gift to the lawyers). By the time the terminus was planned, money was very tight indeed. For all its austerity, some shareholders therefore still protested at the company's 'extravagance in erecting so splendid a station'. Had funds been available, a station hotel would surely have been provided from the start, rather than being awkwardly shunted in next door, without interconnection with the station proper. The hotel eventually cost £30,000 – barely a third of the outlay at St Pancras for furnishing alone, but a burden that could not be justified before the parent station was finished and its trains at last earning a return on the gigantic initial investment.

One way round this constraint was to shuffle off the task of building the station hotel on to a separate, usually subsidiary company. Euston's twin hotels were built in this way, as was the much grander Grosvenor Hotel, a prosperous French Empire design raised in 1860–62 alongside the London, Brighton and South Coast Railway's half of the shared terminus at Victoria. The initial prospectus for the line included a station hotel in the Gothic style, but owing to financial constraints a private company stepped into the breach instead. (Its leading investor was the same very rich contractor who built the new line itself, who shortly afterwards announced his intention to retire, aged just forty-six.) Not until 1899 could the railway afford to buy out this concern and begin to milk the cash cow on its doorstep. The hotel at the South Eastern Railway's Cannon Street terminus was also built by a separate company, as was that erected in 1899 for the Marylebone terminus of the Great Central Railway, the last independent main line to push into the capital before London and Continental Railways' arrival at the remodelled St Pancras in 2007.

The Midland Railway thus did well to retain ownership and control of its hotel at St Pancras. As at King's Cross and Victoria, the terminus building was only the most conspicuous part of an immensely costly project. Some £10,700,000 was spent in bringing the new line from Leicester to London, of which construction contracts for the station swallowed up £435,882. Total expenditure on the hotel was even larger, at £437,335: nine times more than at Paddington, over fourteen times more than at the dowdy Great Northern Hotel next door. Anticipating this gigantic expense, the Midland in turn deferred completion of the building until its trains were running.

Nor did the company have much choice, for the timing of the London extension was exceptionally nerve-racking. The southernmost stages of the line, which proved far costlier than estimated, were started early in 1866. A few months later a crisis on the London capital market briefly kicked bank rates up to a terrifying 10 per cent. The cycle of investment in railway-building, which in the year before had climbed to the highest level for twenty years, now veered steeply downwards. Bankruptcies followed, including the London, Chatham and Dover Railway and the Great Eastern Railway, both dragged down by over-commitment to building new lines, as well as many of the giant contracting firms on which the railways depended for expansion. As the national economy wavered on the edge of a slump, the progress of the Midland's new line became a nail-biting matter. Contractors' bankruptcies were avoided, but two big firms working on the route had to be bailed out by rivals after getting into difficulties. Construction of the train shed lagged as supplies of building materials faltered, until Barlow himself waded in to redirect the contractors' working methods. The size of the labour force at the station site alone gives an idea of how quickly the company was burning through its funds: 1,229 men, 111 horses and 22 steam engines and contractor's locomotives in March 1867. At the same time the Midland was also engaged on the final phases of its Manchester extension and was pushing onwards with plans to raise capital for the staggeringly ambitious Settle and Carlisle line through the northern fells. All this was too much for the shareholders, who secured a vote in 1868 to abandon the Carlisle venture, only to see the necessary Bill rejected by Parliament in the following year.

In these circumstances a grand ceremonial opening for St Pancras might have seemed like a frivolity. Instead, the inauguration was as subdued as could be. A little after midnight on the last day of September in 1868 the night shift from the Midland's booking office walked quietly across the road from King's Cross, where the company had been leasing operating space for the past ten years. (The punitively high charges were yet another incentive to get the new station working as soon as was safely possible.) The trains that ran next day – first arrival, the overnight mail from Leeds at 4.15 a.m.; first departure, the early morning newspaper train to the same city – therefore did so from a part-glazed train shed without even a proper booking office to serve it. One of the timber stages employed to raise the roof still stood inside it, awaiting dismantling.

As for the hotel, the squeeze on funds meant that economies were afoot from the beginning. Among the first casualties was the extra storey indicated on Scott's victorious competition entry of 1865. This was to have contained company offices, allowing the Midland to relocate its headquarters from the line's historic hub at Derby. The financial crisis then postponed the start of work above the foundations until 1868. In the interim Scott revised his drawings to shave £20,000 off the estimates. Not enough; next, he was asked both to make further economies in materials and to devise a way of building the hotel in two stages. The design might have shrunk still further but for the hotel's newly appointed manager, Robert Etzensberger, who insisted in 1872 that it be carried on according to Scott's design. When the first guests booked in on 5 May 1873, the hotel was therefore not yet complete west of the main entrance arch. Not until early in 1877 does the building seem to have been finished inside and out. No ceremony marked either event. Thus both train shed and hotel opened before they were finished, almost furtively.

Scott coped well with these economies, and with other changes that turned the commission into a constantly moving target. In order that the half-built hotel could function until the west wing was completed, some interiors destined for bedrooms had to serve as interim public spaces. The plan had to be reconfigured further once the railway company decided to fill the ground floor between the arrival and departure arches with refreshment rooms and offices rather than the hotel facilities originally intended. This also helps to explain the apparently perverse lack of a grand entrance for rail-borne guests arriving from the station side. The largest of the staircases in the east wing was originally to have done the job, but in the finished building it came down no lower than the floor above. Ornamental features reduced or dropped included the first design for a clock face for the tower and the statues intended to fill the canopied niches of the façade (though not the bronze Britannia, who still hefts her trident from the summit of the solitary east-facing gable). Cheaper materials were substituted too; some parts designed for oak were changed to the softwood known as deal, and Leicestershire slate gave way to the cheaper and less handsome North Welsh kind for roofing less conspicuous areas. Inside, the decoration and furnishing allowed considerable scope for reducing costs without imperilling the all-important mood of luxury and grandeur. None of which was, in the end, enough: at the turn of the year 1873–4 Scott was eased out in favour of the direct employment of the railway's own preferred interior decorating contractor, Messrs Gillow. The architect was not used to this kind of brusque treatment, but he was no prima donna, and a public breach was avoided by both sides.

This process of 'value-engineering' an accepted design before and during construction remains a familiar headache for architects. It was not a sign that the employment of a separate designer was a misconceived luxury. The Midland wanted the grandest of Grand Hotels, not least in order to attract traffic from its longer-established rivals at Euston and King's Cross. It had therefore invited a shortlist of eleven leading architects to compete, of whom Scott was the winner. His design incorporated enough extra features to push the estimated cost £50,000 above that of the second most expensive entry. This prompted protests from two runners-up who had stuck more faithfully to the competition brief; but lavishness was the essence of a design that aimed to put the Midland's rivals in the shade. The company had also drawn the lesson from other London termini, that the hotel should be capable of construction separately from the train shed, and if necessary also later than it. This was one reason why the contract for the hotel foundations was separate from that for the building on top. As for a designer for the train shed, there was no need to pore over the membership list of the Institution of Civil Engineers; the project was well within the expertise of the Midland's own consulting engineer, along with the tunnels, cuttings and viaducts of the new route it served. Having settled on a concept design for the train shed, there was also less scope for the kind of cost-cutting to which the hotel was subjected, which might well have imperilled the stability or longevity of the structure: a final reminder of the different constraints within which architects and engineers normally operate.

But what was the hotel like inside?

5

....

THE MIDLAND GRAND

The railway authorities finally vacated the hotel in the late 1980s, more than half a century after it was turned into offices and renamed St Pancras Chambers. Once the doors closed to guests, it was not long before the wonderful interiors were all but forgotten. Ian Nairn, who could see in Scott's exterior only a clever composition and the competent reckoning of fees, admitted in his *Nairn's London* (1966) that he hadn't actually got inside. One who did was the architectural historian Mark Girouard, who has described slipping in out-of-hours through an unsecured back door, climbing the staircase 'like an explorer stumbling on a deserted temple in the jungle' and finally discovering a way by ladder and trap-door on to the roof. All most irregular; but perhaps no more so than the management's failure to keep up with safety regulations, which triggered the offices' final evacuation on the grounds of a lack of fire escapes.

Despite the flurry of interest in the 1960s, no comprehensive attempt was made to understand how the Victorian hotel was meant to function until the building finally became vacant. The prospect of major restoration and alteration made it essential that the physical fabric was understood, and information on the original purposes of the rooms was also important in deciding their future use and form. The loss of many records and archives has not helped in these tasks; as with the archaeology of earlier centuries, the only evidence sometimes lies in the building itself. What have never been in doubt are its interest and its quality – especially after the restorers' scaffolding came off in 1995 to reveal the newly cleansed red brick and banded stone.

EXPLORATION

By the 1870s the conventions of hotel life were reasonably well established. The first British hotels proper had appeared in the late eighteenth century, in London and in smart resorts such as Buxton. They provided rooms in which to sleep and dine, but – in London at least – normally omitted stabling or coach-booking facilities, which remained the preserve of the coaching inns. The grander type of urban hotel catered for those few who were rich enough to travel by private coach; the smaller type merged indistinguishably into the ranks of the private lodging-house. Finer hotels often included a coffee room open to the public (which for a long time, it seems, meant men only), and a dining-room reserved for the guests. They normally sat around a single table and were expected to converse politely. The Continental habit of dining out in return for a smaller bill was not allowed for; conversely, the prohibition on non-resident guests at dinner ruled out sampling the cuisine at other hotels. Long-term residents or those travelling *en famille* might engage a suite of interconnected rooms, a custom already provided for in the last generation of English coaching-era hotels such as the Queen's at Cheltenham Spa. This practice was especially well established in the United States, where truly gigantic hotels began to appear a decade or so before the first railways came. In other aspects too the story of Britain's grand hotels is essentially one of trying to catch up with the Americans, as will appear.

Many of these conventions are reflected in the planning of the hotel. The establishment was in fact slightly less vast than the exterior suggests, for at platform level everything east of the great departures archway under the western tower was the territory of ordinary travellers and railwaymen. Here were the passengers' refreshment and dining rooms (rented out to the firm of Spiers & Pond, the leading railway caterers of the day), some of the numerous waiting-rooms (classified by sex and ticket class), and sundry railway offices. Behind, placed for ease of access just beyond the departure arch, and forming part of an L-shape angled around the south-western corner of the train shed, was the main booking hall. More waiting rooms lay alongside it. A narrow wing also extended all along the east flank of the train shed, with yet more waiting-rooms, and plenty of lavatories – though possibly never enough, given that trains did not yet include this facility, so that many passengers must have arrived in an advanced state of desperation. All this left just the curved-ended western wedge of the ground floor for hotel use, which forced some of its major rooms up on to the first floor.

This double-decked arrangement was inconvenient in some respects, and Scott has been criticised for it. But the usable extent of the ground floor was not of his choosing: as we have seen, it was determined first by Barlow's placing of the access archways and other railway facilities, then squeezed by the company's decision that the area between the arches would not form part of the hotel after all. So the

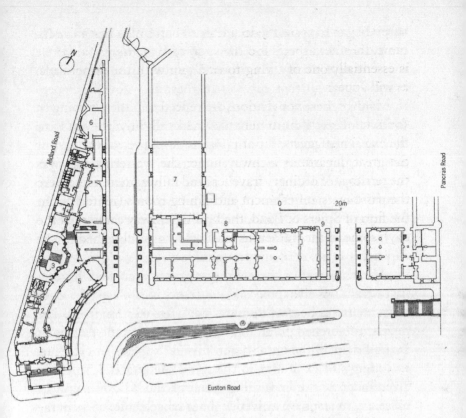

20. A plan of the main floor of the Midland Grand Hotel, before adaptation to return it to hotel use, showing the entrance hall (1), principal corridor (2), main staircase (3), lift (4), coffee room (5), smoking room (6), booking hall (7), hotel entrance from the platform (8), and arrivals arch (9).

surprising thing is not so much that Scott's plan has its faults, but rather that there should be so few of them. What we cannot know is how it compared to the other competition entries, since all that survives of these is a single perspective of the scheme by the architect and design theorist Owen Jones, shown as if from the train-shed end. That the outcome may have been 'steered' from the start is suggested by the way Scott was invited to join the competition at a late stage and his subsequent victory, despite piling in much more than the competition instructions stipulated. Could it also be that the Midland's directors considered his design the best response to the exacting challenges of Barlow's outline plan? The explanations are certainly compatible.

As if to underline the point that guests need not necessarily be train travellers, the main entrance was placed far away from the train shed, on the extreme south-western front. The deep triple-arched porch reaching out towards the pavement is the first place where the rich carving appears in close-up, including shields of arms of England, Ireland and Scotland: a reminder of the expanding reach of the Midland and its allies. Eight steps – no niceties about wheelchair access in the 1870s – ascend from under the porch and into the entrance hall, a room markedly unlike the soothing foyer or lobby of the modern luxury hotel, with its squashy seats for awaiting guests or visitors. The earliest photographs show that much of the space was originally screened off by Gothic-windowed timber partitions for offices, and that a single smallish mat tempered the hardness of the ornate Minton-tiled floor. The room might look not much better than an ordinary booking hall were it not for the luxuriant architectural detailing: a gorgeous twin-arched opening to the corridor ahead, with a fat monolithic column of white-veined green stone on the central pier; alongside it an internal window opening into the porters' office, with enriched tracery like something from a fifteenth-century Venetian palace; and marvellously stylised reliefs of birds on the cross-members of the windows. Like the other architectural carvings, these were the work of Scott's favourite commercial sculptors, Messrs Farmer & Brindley, who performed the same role for him at the Albert Memorial and elsewhere. So the consolations of art were present, even if the frailties of the body were apparently not taken much care of.

As for the painted decoration, this was executed after Scott had lost of control of the interior finishes to the railway's nominees, Messrs Gillow, who were already contracted to supply the hotel furniture. It was overlaid by successive redecorations into the 1900s, without departing drastically from the warm colours and simple foliage patterns of the first phase. Investment and modernisation then tailed off as the Midland Grand slipped inexorably into the second division, followed by years of ossification after the doors closed to the public. The resulting unofficial museum of defunct technologies will be a great challenge to the twenty-first-century operators, who have to decide how many historic decorative schemes to restore or re-create and how much of the rare but obsolete equipment to preserve. One case in point from the entrance hall: the revolving entrance door, supplied from America by the Van Kannel Door Co. in 1899, when it was only the second of its type in London. Some parts of this pioneering installation have survived, and it could theoretically be re-created; but this would be neither the real thing nor an 'original' feature, whatever its interest in terms of building technology and the advance of New World know-how into Europe.

The corridor beyond follows the gentle curve of the wing itself, giving an extra frisson as the foot of the staircase gradually reveals itself at the far end. But some guests would instead have turned into the modest opening to the left, to enter the 'ascending room', alias the 'rising room', elevator or lift. Though novel enough to lack a settled terminology, this perilous-seeming device was already established in London's grand hotels: the Charing Cross and Grosvenor both had one, as did the two biggest non-railway hotels of the early 1860s, the Westminster Palace and the Langham. This was only a little behind the United States, where hydraulically operated lifts on the safety-catch principle pioneered by Elisha Otis were introduced to a New York hotel for the first time in 1859. St Pancras had two passenger lifts and two for goods, arranged in pairs and likewise hydraulically operated, of which the western passenger lift and its goods companion were replaced by electric Otis-type safety fittings in 1891. This in turn was two years after the first American electric lift began operation, and seventeen years before self-closing doors were invented, inevitably also in America. Early lifts therefore required the operator to lock the outer doors on departure, a safety feature that was not extended to the service lifts – as one nocturnally wandering guest discovered to his undoing in 1883.

The habit of going up and down by lift rapidly saw off the phenomenon of the grand full-height hotel staircase, which in most new establishments shrank into a link between ground floor and first floor only. Such was the story at the Savoy, opened on the Thames embankment in the 1880s, which boasted six passenger lifts. Even the spectacle-hotels of contemporary Las Vegas have not sought to revive anything so wasteful of space as the full-height stair, though some sky-scraper-height hotels with atriums soaring up through the middle have appeared around the world since the 1980s. The wonderful staircase at St Pancras therefore comes near the end of a line that can be traced back through domestic architecture to its beginnings in the extravagant palaces of the Baroque era (the Middle Ages never dared this kind of leap into the void). Its effects are achieved by a relatively simple plan: a short, straight flight to a half-landing, then matching arms that sweep back within the semicircular ends of the stair compartment to reach the three upper floors. The magic comes from the giddy cross-views, both up and down, and through the arched column screens to the main landings; from the fall of clear westerly light from the cathedral-height windows; and from the marked narrowing of the flights as the upper floors are reached, so that the initial perception of tight, crowded space gives way to something almost precariously spacious at the very top. All this cannot be captured with justice in any single photograph, which has not prevented the staircase from becoming the iconic interior of the building. In 1995 it also became the first to be wholeheartedly restored, leaving the walls as redecorated in 1901 – crimson, dotted with gold fleurs-de-lys – under the elaborate rib-vault, painted blue and powdered with suns and stars.

Besides its spatial drama and rich colour, the stair is also unforgettable for its means of construction. Every member is immediately legible, from the girders running straight across the void or swerving and criss-crossing under the stone treads and landings to the brackets that arch out from the walls to

21. The hotel staircase in 1998 after restoration of the paintings in the vault. In such a ceremonious setting, Scott's 'honest' display of structural ironwork under the landings was unprecedented.

brace them. Only the topmost flights, where the cumulative load of step upon step is less, are not supported in this way. At first glance the armature seems to be made entirely of iron, but it is not: the sides of the beams are sheathed in panels of dun-coloured fibrous plasterwork. Here is the fulfilment of Scott's programme in the *Remarks* of 1857, which recommended that decorations of brass, plaster, terracotta or even porcelain be added to soften the harshness of exposed iron construction in a building of 'finished character'. Variants of the staircase's plaster panels duly recur on the iron girders crossing the ceilings in several other rooms. Architects had previously been at pains to hide any internal iron beams from the polite gaze, so the staircase shows Scott's courage twice over: as a structure (apparently designed without assistance from an engineer) and as a defiantly explicit expression of structural truth in one of the last places one would expect: a grand hotel.

The use of wrought iron for the balustrades is more conventional, though their taut tiers of scrolls divided by twisted uprights recall ironwork of the Middle Ages rather than the obvious Georgian precedents. The makers were Skidmores of Coventry, another of Scott's favourite suppliers, who also created the marvellous metalwork screens the architect designed for his cathedral restorations. (The one from Hereford, ungratefully expelled in 1967, now shimmers above the entrance hall of the Victoria and Albert Museum.) So here the moving spirit is explicitly medieval, a match for the ornate arched screens to the landings. The newel-posts doubled as gas-lamp stands until about 1885, when a primitive dynamo was attached to one of the boilers and gas mantles gave way to the fitful glimmer of early carbon-filament lamps

– for hotels were avid pioneers of self-generated electricity. Near the bottom the iron balustrade is replaced by close-textured, vaguely Ottoman wooden screens, explained by the former presence in the stairwell of a kiosk selling Turkish coffee, and appearing here like a Saracen with a walk-on part in a medieval mystery play. Another oriental note was struck by the patterns of the vast Wilton Axminster stair carpet, lifted and stowed away only in 1979.

The final touch is provided by the paintings that fill the blind wall-arches just under the vault. One shows the arms of the Midland Railway, the others seated figures of Virtues: not the traditional seven, but a more numerous and more secular crew made up of Humility, Liberality, Chastity, Temperance, Truth, Charity, Patience and Industry. They were painted in 1877 by one of Gillow's men, to designs bought in from the architect Edward William Godwin, who thus acquired an unexpected footnote in the St Pancras story. For Godwin's career exemplifies the flight of the younger generation of designers from the heights of the Gothic Revival, in his case to a spare and sophisticated aesthetic strongly influenced by Japan and the patronage of Whistler and Oscar Wilde (later an unwilling resident of one of Scott's early buildings, as prisoner C.3.3, Reading Gaol). Godwin's life was scandalous too, for he ran off with the actress Ellen Terry, the teenaged wife of the artist G. F. Watts, thus putting himself on the margins of respectable society. Much of his later work was therefore dependent on sympathetic private patrons, including the Earl of Limerick, for whom he designed a sturdy castle at Dromore in Ireland. The clear-lined and austere personifications at St Pancras, with their hints of a Japanese sensibility in the stylised suns and trees of the backgrounds, were actually intended for Dromore. Softer in style and mood is the late Victorian painting that fills a big niche on the first-floor landing: The Garden of Deduit, by Thomas Wallis Hay. This scene of dalliance derives from a late fifteenth-century Flemish illustration of the verse romance the *Roman de la Rose*: another acceptably secular medieval subject for a Neo-Gothic hotel.

The Midland Grand has sometimes been described as a kind of epitome of commercial society, but the adoption of decorations intended for an earl's castle hints at a more nuanced interpretation. Like the gentlemen's clubhouses of the West End, the hotel was a space in which upper and upper-middle classes could consort without uneasiness, whether as guests or visitors: a correlative to the meetings of the railway directorship, when landowners, bankers and salaried managers would sit and debate on equal terms. The background of solid and accomplished design also asserted the unshakeable security of the railway company as an investment, while keeping at a safe distance the more garish decorative styles of theatre, music-hall or gin palace: places the clientèle might well choose to visit, but whose disreputable or *déclassé* associations were not welcome in a first-class hotel.

None of the other interiors can rival the staircase for richness or drama, which is not to say that the public rooms are unimpressive. Two principles governed their planning: the need for access by non-residents, and the division of facilities by sex. Chief among the spaces open to visitors was the hundred-foot-long Coffee Room, placed between the curving ground-floor corridor and the forecourt, and easily accessible from the entrance hall. The wall-shafts here are of polished stone, their capitals carved according to Ruskinian precept with carefully differentiated foliage: fern, pomegranate, vine. Between them span plaster-decorated iron girders like those of the staircase. (More ironwork is hidden within the floors, most of which are of patent concrete and iron construction in order to reduce the risk of fire.) The original painted frieze and the full-height murals that replaced them in the 1900s are both lost, however, and the original concave termination at one end has been screened across with a straight partition.

Beyond the staircase on the north side were a smoking room, a hairdressing room and a billiard room, where this quintessentially Victorian game could be played under the eye of a man employed at ten shillings a week specifically to chalk up the scores (except on Sundays and out of licensing hours, for such was the law). The original use of the individual rooms is not altogether clear, partly because the two-phase construction required some functions to migrate from the east wing after a few years, partly because the sources contradict one another. But there is no question that the ground floor was decidedly masculine in character.

The ladies' domain was on the floor above: notably a crescent-shaped dining room, and a lounge or coffee room leading off it and facing the main road. The dining room was made so large at the insistence of the manager, Robert Etzensberger, a veteran of the Venetian hotel trade and of catering on the Nile steamers; Scott's early drawings show a series of smaller rooms instead. Beyond is the Ladies' Coffee Room, a splendid if oddly shaped interior, subdivided by a round-arched arcade on paired columns of red granite from Shap in Westmorland. Some time after 1895 it was equipped with the 'Electrophone', a one-way telephone subscription with an apparatus that allowed up to eight people to listen in to live concerts, public speeches and church services. At about the same time the space appears to have been re-designated a Ladies' Smoking Room, a bold move at a time when the New Woman was not a universally acceptable figure. Early photographs also show how the space was thrown open in summer to an outside terrace over the porch, protected by an awning and set about with potted plants. And yet the noise of horses' hooves and iron-hooped wheels must have been thunderous, even after the company paid in 1881 for the rubber-jointed wooden blocks already used to deaden noise on the hotel approach road to be extended out into the public highway. To imagine a fashionable lady of 1900 in this room, straining to decode the muffled chords of Wagner or Debussy above the roar of horseshoes and cartwheels, is to feel the poignancy of the gulf between the present and the not so distant past.

No less evocative of a lost age are some of the service rooms and utilities, which have survived because no one thought it worthwhile replacing them. Several of the lavatories opening off the corridors are still lined in the beautiful maroon-and-white tiles specially designed for the building by the Minton firm, and the hotel also preserves some early free-standing ceramic water closets, receptacles normally among the first victims of any refurbishment programme. Other exceptional relics include intact fire-hydrant cabinets and giant radiators in the same corridors. The latter were originally heated by steam, which meant that perforated wooden cases had to be provided to save guests from inadvertent burns. Scott wanted to make more extensive use of central heating, but cost constraints meant that most rooms were equipped with cheaper open fireplaces instead, to a total of many hundreds. The removal from their chimneys of the tall patent cowls added after 1885 to help carry the smoke clear of the building was one of the subtler improvements of the external restoration in the 1990s.

Open fireplaces were therefore standard in the guests' rooms, most of which were reached from the cathedral-length corridors extending from each main landing (carried across the entrance arches at first-floor level, it will be remembered, by cast-iron enclosed bridges of audacious design). The original doors mostly survive: exceptionally wide to modern eyes, with flattened Gothic mouldings and spidery timber-traceried fanlights above them to allow a little borrowed light into the corridors. Some of the rooms behind were arranged into suites, others were singles of the type most familiar today. Cheaper accommodation was on the upper floors: despite the presence of a lift, the old inverse relationship between the degree of prestige and the number of stairs that needed to be climbed above the first floor was still firmly in operation. Aspect mattered too, and more so than usual, for much of the northern side was obscured by the train shed.

Rooms were also graduated by quality of furnishings and facilities, with a care that seems obsessive even when one remembers how inescapable were such markers of status and class in the 1870s. As the surviving account books show, the best rooms mostly had furniture of oak or walnut. Some also had painted ceilings to designs supplied by Scott and executed by the German-born decorative artist Frederick Sang. On the second floor the furniture was of oak or teak; on the third floor, mahogany; on the fourth floor, ash. As photographs show, the style of these pieces was not at all Gothic, but a watered-down version of the spindly Japanesey aesthetic pio-

22. A sitting room in one of the Midland Grand's larger suites, photographed in 1876. The decorations and furnishings mostly avoid explicitly medieval forms in favour of the eclectic-cum-Aesthetic fashions of the day.

neered by Godwin and his fellow spirits. Passages on floors three and four had Brussels carpets edged with linoleum, instead of the costlier Axminsters on the levels below. On the fifth floor – the upper of the two storeys fitted into the huge roof – the floors had mere coconut matting, and the furniture was softwood with an oak-effect finish. (The idea has taken hold that staff dormitories entirely filled these roof storeys, but the records and plans indicate that much of the space was actually divided into small bedrooms, for guests of more modest means.) Eight-inch-dial clocks costing £25 each kept time in the best rooms, but those supplied to 'inferior bed-rooms' cost just £8. Early views show vases of various size and elaboration flanking them on the overmantels, for a bare mantelpiece would have been an affront to decorum even in a hotel. Crockery was graduated too, from earthenware in the refreshment rooms to Royal Worcester for the best interiors, such as the commode now preserved at the Midland Railway Study Centre at Derby: a necessary object, given the remoteness of many rooms from a lavatory. Even the pianos available for use in the best sitting-rooms were differently ranked: one grand, four oblique, five cottage. Windows were hung with silken or woollen curtains and roll-up 'pinoleum blinds' made of painted softwood slats. Such indulgences all showed up in the tariff, as an American visitor of simpler tastes complained in 1882 ('One does not desire to sleep amid purple and gold').

Missing from this list of facilities is the bathroom, *de rigueur* in the best American establishments but much less frequently encountered in Victorian Britain. At the Midland Grand just nine were provided initially, all reached from the corridors rather than directly from the suites. If this figure sounds astonishingly low, that is partly because we have forgotten the old practice of washing using movable furnishings – hip-baths and wash-basins – rather than plumbed-in fittings. In a Victorian hotel the normal thing was to bathe in one's own room in just such a hip-bath, using hot water brought by the chambermaid; the bath was often stowed under the bed when not in use.

Two shillings was a common charge for this service. Most hotels also added a daily 'attendance charge' of a shilling for the maid and for the waiter at dinner, and another sixpence for the boot-black. Candles incurred a traditional shilling-and-sixpence levy on top of that, and a further charge was imposed to put a fire in the grate. To the guest in the suite with the grand piano such surcharges would have counted for little, but the incremental billing was a deterrent to travellers of more modest means; hence the statement in Charles Dickens junior's *Dictionary of London* of 1879, that railway hotels may prove expensive for 'people who do not understand hotel life'. It also contributed to the immediate success of Frederick Gordon's new mid-priced hotels of the 1880s – the decade when specialist companies took over from the railways as London's chief hotel builders – where all-in bills were the custom from the outset. The Midland seems to have abolished the attendance tariff at about the same time. Here was another step away from the old days before the railway, when to travel at all was to risk being fleeced at every turn by poor provisions and spurious surcharges.

The Gordon hotels constituted one of Britain's first hotel chains, of the kind now inescapable around the world. The major railway companies also owned more than one hotel, but the Midland and its General Manager, Sir James

Allport, were unusual in their enthusiasm for them, building or acquiring large establishments in most of the bigger cities served. This was partly a consequence of the company's need to compete with older rivals by offering higher standards of comfort and customer care, a theme that recurs in the next chapter. Though it went on to build more up-to-date hotels – the one in sooty Manchester even had an early form of air-conditioning by means of linen filters – London's remained the Midland's flagship. It was proudly represented in its advertisements and publicity pictures, sometimes with the extra floor originally proposed by Scott, an outrageous lie designed solely to make the building look even bigger.

All these hotels were managed from the mid 1880s by William Towle, whose offices filled the topmost storey of the Midland Grand's west tower. A gifted hotelier and administrator, Towle entered the trade at the Midland Hotel at Derby aged fifteen and retired, knighted, in 1914 (after which his two sons took over, one of whom continued in post until 1944, managing what had become the largest hotel chain in Europe). Despite burdensome wider responsibilities, which included the company's refreshment rooms and dining cars, Towle's management was decidedly of the hands-on school. His surviving memos include such minutiae as the adequate cooking of barley grains in the Scotch broth and the correct mixing of the inconceivably nasty-sounding beverage of cold Bovril and soda. His wife meanwhile supervised the housekeeping and the railway's large female staff, housekeeping being one of the few managerial occupations normally undertaken by women in Victorian Britain.

23. The Midland Grand as Scott originally designed it, as dishonestly represented in subsequent company publicity. The intended extra floor would have made the frontage still more overpowering, but would also have blunted the soaring effect of the towers. The openings in the retaining wall of the terrace now serve an enlarged concourse for the Underground station.

It will be clear by now how far the Midland Grand depended for its functioning on massed labour, much of which was normally kept discreetly out of sight. So far we have been exploring as members of the élite. Turn the wheel of fortune the other way, and different spaces and storeys come into focus.

Many of the essential services were swallowed by the basement, including the boiler rooms, kitchens and laundry. Kitchens were in the west wing, where their windows appear low down on the wall facing Midland Road. Scott had no prior experience of designing a hotel, so their equipment was specified by the contracting supplier. Frederick Williams has left a vivid if hyperbolic account of what they were like on his visit in 1876. Floors were strewn with sawdust, and everywhere – of course – 'order, cleanliness and method seemed to reign supreme'. There was specialised storage space aplenty; Williams noted especially the bottling room (the hotel bottled much of the wine it served, besides blending its own tea and coffee), the many cellars piled with casks, and the plate room, where the expected silverware was set out ready for use. The kitchen proper was equipped with iron cupboards and a giant fire 'in front of which a couple of dozen joints could be cooked at once'. Which they doubtless often were; for roast meat at dinner, like soup, was a normal component of the tariff, and à la carte dining did not become the norm in British hotels until the next century. Orders came by ticket down a lift, and servings were dispatched by the same route. In the refectory room Williams found the staff busy preparing a wedding breakfast, including 'the breasts of a whole covey of partridges ... in a rounded glistering tomb of jelly'. A separate room housed iron steam-chests for vegetables, and steam was also made much use of in the laundry. This was a very advanced installation, with a steam-heated washing machine six feet in diameter which could boil up to three thousand pieces of linen a day. These then passed via a centrifugal wringer and two steam mangles with heated rollers into a steam-heated airing room to finish them off – a space that Williams found too sweltering to pass beyond the threshold.

Incoming dirty laundry came down from the bedroom floors through chutes placed off each corridor just beyond the landing. Coal and goods lifts, operated by hand on the dumb-waiter principle, were housed alongside them. Behind the lift shafts on each floor, linked vertically by back stairs, was a capacious maids' room, equipped with hot running water from the basement boilers and with an array of electric bells for summons to the guests' chambers. Both staff and goods could thus circulate between floors out of sight of the guests, emerging only for the final, horizontal stages along the corridors. Communication between storeys was by means of speaking tubes, set likewise alongside the service lifts. All these facilities were grouped vertically, like the service cores of modern steel- or concrete-framed buildings. There was also a sealed shaft for 'dust', which would have included ashes from the hundreds of fires, and even a tube for the stream of outgoing letters: the usual method of public and private communication in the days before telephones, when the penny post within central London would normally achieve delivery later the same day. These passed via a letter office on each floor, where little lead weights were attached to ensure that they did not get stuck on the way down.

The number of personnel required to operate this great

inhabited machine varied according to season, as at any large hotel today, and also from day to day over the week. The figures recorded on census Sunday in 1881 – 91 guests, 115 resident staff – therefore may not be representative. Ten years later the staff headcount was 145. (The company also tried to limit unproductive employment by drafting employees between the various hotels of the Midland system.) Some were assigned to dormitories in the topmost roof storey, which were divided by sex and reached by separate staircases to prevent improper intercommunication. Rooms in the basement provided sleeping space for most of the remainder.

It is not easy for the twenty-first-century traveller to appreciate the daily drudgery of a hotel regime dependent on coal fires, hand-sweeping, and cleaning without detergents. To try to enter imaginatively into the lives of the staff, moving constantly on and off shift from their quarters up above the smoky rooftops or below street level, is a harder challenge still. After the splendours of the public rooms, the bleakness of these zones comes as a jolt to the modern explorer. But contemporaries would have had other standards of comparison: the servants' dormitories within the roofspaces of country houses, the comfortless spaces of barracks and police lodging-houses, the stifling crew's quarters of merchant and naval ships. Railway employment resembled these forms of service in the surrender of autonomy in return for security, perhaps a uniform, and certainly some prospect of promotion, with the extra benefits of cut-price travel and occasional treats and excursions. Life in a railway hotel added to this balance sheet the surrender of much privacy in return for accommodation, which in this case extended to some common-rooms down in the basement, including a bar or tap-room. The first generations of staff also included numerous Germans and Swiss, many of whom must have hoped to make profitable use of their hoteliers' English on return to their home countries. The omnipresence of hierarchy, discipline and petty regulation went without saying, enforced by fines docked from wages, a borrowing from the factory system. For instance, in the 1900s any Midland Grand employee caught eating an apple was fined threepence. But if you did not like the regime, you could walk out and seek a better place in another hotel, an option not so easily available to the soldier or sailor.

What those employees' lives were like is much less well documented than the toils of engineers and locomotive men, for which railway enthusiasts have long provided a rapt audience. Even so, a few memoirs were recorded in the middle decades of the last century. P. W. Smith started work as a fifteen-year-old page in 1898, and earned a tip the following year by demonstrating the new revolving door to the satisfaction of the local fire officer. On another occasion he was sent with a note to an imminently departing express in the station, the conductor of which informed him that he would henceforth be working as a dining-car pantry boy and would spend the night in the staff hostel in Glasgow (Smith managed to get his old post back after a month). Another former page recalled carrying letters to Sir William Towle's suburban residence on Sunday mornings, waiting at the chief's bedside for any replies. Contemporary records provide other glimpses, such as the *Railway Magazine*'s account of the multilingual porter identified in 1931 at Leeds station (seven tongues, including Arabic and Hindi), who was promptly reassigned to the new Continental enquiry bureau at St Pancras. Further accounts come via oral tradition. The mother of one recent visitor was working as a chambermaid during the nocturnal air raid of 17 February 1918, when twenty people sheltering near the departure arch were killed by a single bomb; the maid was shocked just as much by the sight of a thoroughly panicked lady guest clad only in a nightgown.

Whatever their frustrations may have been, the lives of the hotel's staff were enviable by the standards of some of Victorian London's other temporary residents. Most of these would have stayed in lodgings, a term extending from respectable comfort to cramming into the poorest type of house. Chronic overcrowding had ended after the Common Lodging House Act of 1852, which gave the Metropolitan Police powers to enforce minimum standards within the capital. Even so, the slum literature of the years when the Midland Grand was under construction still contains much to chill the blood. Typical is Blanchard Jerrold's nocturnal tour of the East End in 1872, safely accompanied by a super-intendent from Whitechapel police station, 'threading the long passages of deal boards that separate the twopenny beds of the lodgers ... In one box an old man is dying of asthma; in another two fine baby boys are interlaced, sleeping till their mother brings them home some supper from the hard streets.' Private philanthropic undertakings by George Peabody and others supplied a few enclaves of model housing aimed at the better-off worker, but the politics of Victorian housing meant that little could be done for the homeless and displaced while they remained so very poor. Even the Salvation Army's hostel in Southwark, opened in 1891, charged fourpence a night for one of the three or four beds in each of its matchboarded cubicles, with another penny for soup and bread: about one twenty-fifth of the highest tariff at the Midland Grand, but double the rate noted by Jerrold in Whitechapel.

Though the railways made travel possible for the masses, it would take wider social changes before the ordinary person could expect to stay in anything so select as a hotel. The Midland Grand and its train shed are therefore divided by more than questions of style and design. The platforms were an extension of public space, where the classes mixed and mingled in ways beloved of Royal Academicians and the cartoonists of *Punch*. Within the hotel, hierarchy and social stratification ruled. The physical distance of the Midland Grand from the public street echoed this social barrier, just as the 'far-reaching prospects' from its windows, as the railway's *Official Guide* was pleased to put it, corresponded to the elevated status of its guests. And while the British hotel is sometimes described as enjoying its golden age in Victorian and Edwardian times, the caveat also holds true: perceptions of a golden age depend on who has charge of the gold.

DEGENERATION

Why did the hotel close in 1935? A vague idea still circulates that it had simply become out of its time, an enchanted Pre-Raphaelite castle stranded among Odeons and streamliners. In this spirit, not long after the Second World War, John Betjeman gloomily prophesied its destruction as 'too beautiful and too romantic to survive'.

This certainly reflects the collapse in official esteem for Victorian Gothic, but it does not explain the specific circumstances in which the decision was made. A rueful remark by the chairman of the Gordon Hotel Company in 1928 offers a surer clue: hotels were like battleships, obsolete after twenty years. The occasion was the conversion to offices of the company's Grand Hotel in Trafalgar Square. The same fate was shared between 1920 and the 1940s by a good many other once lustrous names, including London's first three big non-railway hotels: the Westminster Palace, the Buckingham Palace and the Langham in Portland Place (now a grand hotel again). Size was no defence; demolition overtook the Hotel Cecil on the Strand, the largest in Britain when new, but by the 1930s worth less than the redevelopment value of its site. All of these were built between the 1860s and the 1880s and therefore had to compete with the many splendid hotels built subsequently; in 1913 it was estimated that London had spent £10 million on hotels over the previous decade alone. Star items on this bill included the new Ritz in Piccadilly and the unstinting modernisation of the Savoy, London's only Victorian grand hotel that has stayed consistently in the first rank. Here the changes included infilling the balconies facing the river, which released enough space inside to allow American-style en suite bathrooms to be installed in the best apartments.

Few of these inter-war casualties were railway-owned. Such hotels could draw on a solid market of travellers attracted by their convenience – including free conveyance of luggage from the station – and their reputation for dependability. Nor were such handicaps as the shortage of plumbing truly insuperable; after all, the Great Western had successfully modernised its even older hotel at Paddington in 1931 (when the exterior was cruelly shaved of ornament in a gesture towards the jazz age). Had the Midland Railway preserved its independent existence, something similar would surely have happened at St Pancras, which as late as 1923 was one of only two railway hotels to earn a star in Baedeker's *London Guide*. Instead, the company was subsumed in that year into the London, Midland and Scottish Railway, which meant that the old rival at Euston became the hotel's elder stepsister. Profits from the two hotels initially marched in step, but by the early 1930s Euston was well ahead.

An unexpected glimpse of the Midland Grand's decline during these years can be had from a humorous letter of 1928 by the artist Paul Nash, whose London flat was a few streets away. Lacking a wireless set, Nash and his wife arranged to listen to the broadcast of a friend's radio play in a corner of the hotel's 'reading-room' (the old Ladies' Coffee Room?). Their careful instructions were in vain: it took half an hour for the bumbling and occasionally sarcastic staff to get the equipment working – a sorry come-down from the palmy days of the Electrophone – and even the specially ordered coffee tasted poisonous. Nash seems to have forgiven the establishment, for soon afterwards he made it the subject of one of his most important canvases, *Northern Adventure*. In this dream-like transformation of the view from his window a scaffolded hoarding screens the station's access ramp and a version of the departures arch. Its pointed summit is shown rounded off, as if in homage to the ambiguous viaducts and arcades in the works of Nash's latest discovery, the Italian 'metaphysical' painter Giorgio di Chirico. Italianised English Neo-Gothic, transfigured under the influence of Italian *avanguardismo*: a Northern Adventure indeed.

In 1933 the chairman of the company, Sir Josiah (later Lord) Stamp, aired the St Pancras dilemma at the annual dinner address of the Royal Institute of British Architects.

24. *Northern Adventure*, by Paul Nash (1928). The gate pier and access ramp
with its pedestrian steps are unmistakable. Beyond is the departures arch,
lightly disguised by means of a rounded top.

Though he could still admire it as a masterpiece of its age, the hotel was 'completely obsolete and hopeless' as such, and worse than useless as offices. If kept, it would be a dead loss economically; if demolished, its replacement would be just as unfashionable in another sixty years. Of course, the dead-loss option won the day. The company's hotels office took over the commercial rooms, while the roof storeys became a hostel for cleaning ladies. Three porters were also deputed to meet arrivals and steer them towards the special bus to the Euston Hotel, and away from the competitor at King's Cross. It was an ignominious turn for an establishment described when new as 'the most perfect in every possible respect in the world'. However, the new order was also a blessing, freezing the destruction of the historic interiors or masking them behind flimsy partitions and suspended ceilings. At Paddington the hotel preserves almost nothing from the age of Brunel; at St Pancras the romance of Victorian modernity lives on into the twenty-first century.

6

....

THE RAILWAY WORLD

Railways were born nearly three hundred miles north of St Pancras, in the coal-mining districts of Northumberland and County Durham. Mines across Europe already used simple wooden rails to guide mineral trucks, both underground and for carrying cargoes from mine to shipping point. By replacing wood with iron, running the wagon wheels along the tops of the rails instead of between them (kept in place by flanges on the wheels' inner edges), and hauling trains by steam locomotives rather than horse-power, manpower or gravity, the modern railway was born. The Stockton and Darlington railway (1825) was the first to do all these things, though its passenger trains were at first horse-drawn; the more ambitious Liverpool and Manchester Railway (1830) was the first major line to use steam haulage for all trains from the outset.

Early passengers struggled to express to the uninitiated how astonishingly different the world looked from a railway carriage in a state of locomotion. 'The objects we passed were metamorphosed into every imaginable caricature of form ... it seemed as if gates, posts, rails and all were starting from their holds and dancing to greet our arrival.' Thus one traveller in 1830, from the opening fortnight's operation of the Liverpool and Manchester. That the maximum velocity barely rose above thirty miles per hour mattered not at all: this

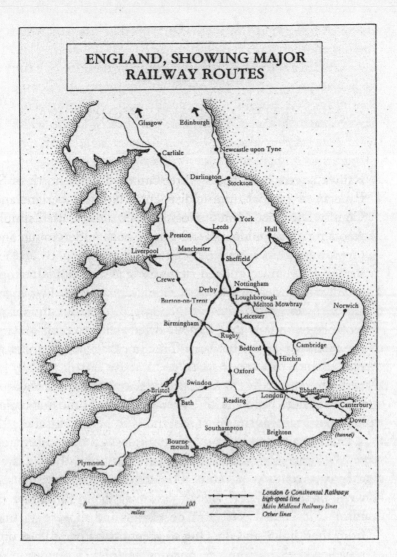

ENGLAND, SHOWING MAJOR RAILWAY ROUTES

Glasgow
Edinburgh
Carlisle
Newcastle upon Tyne
Darlington
Stockton
York
Leeds
Hull
Preston
Liverpool
Manchester
Sheffield
Crewe
Nottingham
Derby
Loughborough
Burton-on-Trent
Melton Mowbray
Norwich
Leicester
Birmingham
Rugby
Cambridge
Bedford
Hitchin
Oxford
Swindon
London
Ebbsfleet
Bristol
Canterbury
Bath
Reading
Dover
Southampton
Brighton
(tunnel)
Bourne-mouth
Plymouth

London & Continental Railways
high-speed line
Main Midland Railway lines
Other lines

0   100
miles

25. A map of selected British railways, including the Midland's main lines and those of its competitors: a modest proportion of more than 20,000 route miles built between 1825 and 1914.

was much faster than anyone had travelled before, and when crossing another train the closing speed was doubled – 'and you are left in a state of excitement not to be described'. Even the landscape traversed was no longer the same. As George Eliot witnessed, 'the hills are cut through, or the breaches between them spanned, we choose our level, and the white steam-pennon flies along it.' For mile after mile these new cuttings and embankments confined or exalted views once determined prosaically by contour-bound roads and lanes. Tunnels made sudden, frightening interruptions, in which the noise of the train was hideously amplified and all daylight snatched away. It was a parallel world, bound by its own rules and by-laws, and in Britain it grew with dizzying speed: five thousand route-miles opened between 1846 and 1852 alone. The railways' terms of operation changed too, from a scattering of disconnected lines in the early 1830s to a national network largely made up of about fifteen major companies by the 1860s. Relations between these big firms varied from cordial alliance through local truce to active hostility. They also shifted repeatedly as new lines were opened or annexed and new services begun in the hope of drawing traffic away from rivals. This was the spirit in which the Midland undertook a new main line to London from places that had been served by other companies (not always very directly) for a quarter of a century or more. The station buildings at St Pancras should finally be understood as players in this wider drama.

THE MIDLAND INVASION

The Midland stands out from the other big Victorian railway

companies for the way in which it grew from a regional outfit into a national one, largely by means of the enterprising construction of new lines. The company's name dates from 1844, when three moderate-sized railways with a shared junction at Derby put aside their rivalries in favour of amalgamation. The new chairman was the plausible George Hudson, 'the Railway King', whose interests included stakes in several other lines. All looked rosy for the Midland at this point, for its system included part of the only railway route to York and the north, by means of a junction at Rugby with the London and Birmingham's line to Euston. However, the end of this monopoly was soon in sight: in 1846 the Great Northern Railway was enacted, on a more direct course between York and its new terminus at King's Cross. The newcomer was one of the more successful promotions of the 'Railway Mania' of 1844–7, a classic bubble in which railway shares took on the false lustre of licences to print money and hosts of extravagant and contradictory schemes contended for the capital of the propertied classes. Hudson managed one strategic master-stroke during this heady time by absorbing the new railway from Birmingham to Bristol into the Midland's system. When the bubble burst, however, the company still had no line of its own to London, and a bad odour was emanating from its account books. Hudson's chairmanship ended ignominiously soon after.

To allow its trains to reach the capital, the Midland therefore had no choice but to continue its costly access payments to the London and North Western Railway, the successor company to the London and Birmingham, on the line to Euston. Things improved somewhat after 1858, thanks to the Midland's new route connecting Leicester with Hitchin in

Hertfordshire, where it joined Great Northern rails for the final leg to King's Cross. This also allowed the Midland to establish its own London goods depot alongside that of the host company, a little way up the line from the terminus. The new route entailed expensive access charges too, however, and both host companies were prone to keep the Midland's trains waiting when their own traffic was especially heavy. On one occasion so many Midland coal trains were backed up at Rugby that they stretched for five miles and deliveries had to be cancelled. The company owed its very origin to the eagerness of landlocked coal-owners in the heart of England to find new markets in the south, so this kind of bottlenecking was no small matter. Amalgamation and heavy investment in track-widening might have sorted out much of the trouble, but satisfactory terms could not be agreed. Each host company also attempted at different times to absorb the Midland, only to be stymied by Parliament, which remained highly suspicious of anything that seemed to restrict competition.

The nadir came during the London Exhibition of the summer of 1862, when the Great Northern forced some of the Midland's excursion passengers – becrinolined ladies not excluded – to climb up into their carriages from the sidings because the station proper was too full. Enough was enough: the Midland resolved in the same year that only a separate line of its own would do. The new route was to run south from Bedford for 49 miles, to a new London terminus alongside that of its unsatisfactory partner. So streamlined had the process of railway legislation become by the 1860s that the act to build this extension passed just eight months later, for all that the Great Northern and the London and North Western joined with other interested parties in petitioning against it.

This brief account may give the impression that the Midland was the plucky underdog, struggling against selfish neighbours for a fair share of the London feast. Viewed from other angles, however, Sir James Allport's railway company was perhaps the most ruthlessly invasive of all. Acting alone or ganging up with other lines, it repeatedly muscled in on areas already supplied with services and stations, sometimes by more than one rival railway. Through the 1860s and 1870s the company name became steadily less appropriate as these new trunk lines snaked outwards from its historic heartland, until Manchester, London, Bournemouth and Carlisle were all 'Midland' destinations. The last of these lines, blasted across the western flank of the Pennines to allow the Midland to run through from Leeds and on into Scotland, remains the highest and most spectacular main line in England. Williams's company history of 1876 was pretty belligerent about all this: the London and North Western's policy is summarised as being 'by open attack and by secret treaties, to sap the resources of the Midland and to draw around it a cincture which should cripple it in every limb'. The mixed metaphors from war, statecraft and biology are telling; the Midland is at once a living organism seeking natural growth and an innocent nation-state subjected to the sinister machinations of a rival power.

Conflicts of this kind followed inevitably from the state's refusal to do much more than impose a modest framework of regulation on the industry. The Railway Mania saw the consequences at their lunatic height: at one point 815 railway ventures were before Parliament, costed at a total of six times the national annual expenditure. It was quite different abroad, where the entire network was sometimes centrally planned from the beginning, as in Belgium. Likewise, the railway approaches to Paris were determined by the state on strategic grounds. The French capital ended up with eight railway termini, but fully fifteen were forced into the fabric of London, many of which offered competing services. By 1880 the only large towns without a choice of routes to the metropolis were Bristol, Hull and Newcastle. The lavishness of St Pancras should be understood as a response to this embarrassment of choice. Since all the major towns it served were already accessible from London via long-established rival routes, Allport knew that the company had to work harder to tempt passengers away. The splendiferous terminus and hotel, planted next to dowdy old King's Cross like the palace of a triumphant invader, were meant as both an advertisement and a lure. (In addition, a large rail-served goods depot took shape immediately to the west, planned and built by the Midland in connection with its new terminus; since the 1990s the red-brick compound of the British Library has occupied the site.)

As if to underscore the association with the home territory, the station's contractors used materials sourced almost entirely within the Midland system. Except for its gigantic size, the frontage building would therefore look quite at home in Victorian Leicester or Nottingham. The pressed red bricks of its walls were made in the latter city by Mr Gripper to his own patent, supplemented on the less conspicuous side elevations by cheaper bricks from Loughborough. The Mansfield, Ancaster and Ketton stone dressings were all quarried in the Midland's home counties too, as were the greeny-grey Leicestershire slates used on most of the roofs, while the Butterley ironworks which fabricated the train shed was a long-established Derbyshire concern. Of the chief exterior materials, only the polished granite shafts and the bricks used for the arches came from outside the Midland's territory. This pattern of supply reflected the ways in which the railways' tariff structure shaped the national markets for their cargoes. It commonly cost less to send goods by a single company than to transport them less far by means of two or more rival lines; for example, South Welsh coal was carried for hundreds of miles through the Great Western empire even when supplies no less good could be had from a rival line's territory in an adjacent county. It is therefore too simple to say that the railways created a national market; the walls of St Pancras demonstrate instead the distorting influence of preferential rates within the various companies' home territories.

Associations of this kind helped subtly to establish the character of the company in the public mind, along with standardisation of such things as station nameboards, train liveries and military-style uniforms for staff. These nuances mattered more than ever after the 1870s, when the basis of competition for passengers shifted away from price and rivalrous route-building towards enhanced levels of comfort and service. St Pancras in its splendour therefore represents a late flourish of the great age of railway building. (The last wholly new terminus in London – as noted in Chapter 4 – was the Great Central Railway's at Marylebone, opened in 1899 to serve a superfluous new main line through the midlands: an apologetic and obscurely placed building, demoted to suburban status in the 1960s.) But Allport also realised that fine buildings were not enough on their own; to win and retain custom from its competitors the company needed to shake up the very terms on which people travelled. In this sense St Pancras was also a harbinger of the future.

TRAVEL BY MIDLAND

The carriages that trundled in and out of St Pancras in its earliest years followed the prevailing British classification into first, second and third classes. The last was made universal by Gladstone's Railway Act of 1844, which also enforced a standard cheap rate and required even third-class carriages to be protected by a roof. These 'Parliamentary' services commonly ran as slower and segregated trains, often at unsocial times. Nevertheless, they signalled the arrival of the railways as a means of transport within reach of all but the poorest.

The Midland upset this apple cart twice over. In 1872 it decreed that third-class carriages should be included in every train it ran. Then, from the first day of 1875, it did away with second class altogether, and upgraded its thirds to match their standard. This meant upholstered seats instead of bare wooden ones, full-height compartment divisions rather than back-to-back benches, and footwarmers in season (built-in steam heating began to appear only in the 1890s). First-class fares were reduced to the old second-class rates in order to preserve the differential.

The consequences included an extra four million passenger journeys a year for the company, valuable simplifications to paperwork and operation, and much huffing and puffing from competitors – who gradually followed suit none the less – and from the press. What particularly rankled was the shock to the assumption that society fell naturally into three classes. One paper warned sternly that 'A democratic and

26. The challenges of early railway travel, captured in one of Honoré
Daumier's lithographs for *Le Charivari* on the opening of the Paris–Orléans
line in 1843. Red-hot cinders from the engine were another hazard. Such
scenes soon vanished from Britain thanks to Gladstone's far-sighted
Railway Act of 1844, which made covered carriages compulsory even for
third-class passengers.

social revolution seems to be looming in the railway future', connoting 'the excision of the great middle class from English society'. The *Daily Telegraph* noted more level-headedly that the only losers were first-class passengers afflicted with status anxiety: 'The real sufferers are those poor fellows the rich.' Matters of comfort apart, the equalisation of journey times was of huge benefit to the working class, as Allport remarked:

> *When the rich man travels, or if he lies in bed all day, his capital remains undiminished and perhaps his income flows in all the same. But when a poor man travels he has not only to pay his fare but to sink his capital, for his time is his capital; and if he now consumes only five hours instead of ten in making a journey, he has saved five hours of time for useful labour – useful to himself, his family, and to society.*

The implicit claim that what's good for the company is good for the customer anticipates the self-interested boasts of today's cheap-flight magnates, but it is nice to find the Midland's General Manager using language straight out of *Das Kapital* in which to make it.

The Marxist cultural critic could also puzzle over the contrast between this levelling-up for the ordinary traveller and the finely graduated and priced facilities offered at the Midland Grand. It is almost as if the company expected that arriving passengers would want to recalibrate their position on the social scale as soon as they were inside. In some cases this may not have been far from the truth, for railways had always been disruptive of old ideas of hierarchy in the sharing of space. Many of the old carriage-owning élite thoroughly resented having to travel in the company of strangers, perhaps for the first time on land. A few diehards such as the first Duke of Wellington and the pathologically reclusive fifth Duke of Portland persisted in travelling within their own private coaches, which were trundled on to flat wagons and hitched to a normal passenger train. Conversely, some railway companies were dismayed to find that people who could afford better chose to travel third and save the difference. The Manchester and Leeds was even reported to have dumped sweeps' soot in its third-class carriages as a deterrent to the well-dressed.

Such hierarchical assumptions were set aside once cheap travel proved to be the companies' best source of growth. By 1860 third-class receipts exceeded those from the two better classes combined; by 1900 they made up three-quarters of the yield; by 1913 ninety-six journeys in every hundred were third class. A combination of Parliamentary intervention and company rivalry, spurred on by the Midland, had created an unprecedentedly democratic system of transport without erasing every distinction of wealth and class.

Class anxiety on the railway is the subject of some fun in H. G. Wells's novel *Kipps* (1905). The hero, a dim draper's assistant enriched by an unexpected legacy, travels up to London from Kent on a three-class corridor train:

> *he forgot his troubles for a time in the wonders of this modern substitute for railway compartments. He went from the non-smoking to the smoking carriage, and smoked a cigarette, and strayed from his second-class carriage to a first and back.*

A fish out of water in the capital, he cheers up after running into a childhood friend, and travels home with him by third-class Underground. Later Kipps elopes from Kent with the same friend's sister – but the couple go first-class up to London.

The interconnected carriages which struck Kipps as so novel can also be traced back to the Midland. They first appeared in the shape of the Pullman saloons that Allport imported from America in 1874, which were linked by gangways between open-sided platforms of the kind familiar from a hundred celluloid Westerns. Other amenities included lavatories and wheels mounted on well-sprung pivoting bogies: more instances of American superiority in matters of convenience and comfort. Even so, it took more than a quarter of a century for carriages with lavatories, bogies and gangway connections (enclosed ones, in view of the British climate) to become general on long-distance trains. Interlinked carriages also made it possible for trains to include dining or refreshment cars, so that the ritual of passengers cramming down lamentably inferior food and drink during strictly timetabled refreshment stops began to disappear. Other conventions died harder: coaches made up entirely of separate compartments, each accessible only by a single door on either side, were still being built in the 1950s and still creaking around the suburbs of south London in the early 1980s. Their withdrawal stilled the echoes from a century and a half before, when what was effectively a row of road-coach bodies was spliced together on long chassis for the first time, and the railway carriage was born.

All this is enough to show how far the experience of long-distance train travel changed between the opening of St Pancras and the 1900s – much more so than it did between, say, the 1900s and 1950s. The full cost of these improvements was not apparent to the ordinary passenger. The better-equipped new trains were more expensive to build, and also heavier, so that more powerful and coal-hungry locomotives were needed to pull them. The enhanced signalling, track-work and brakes that allowed the trains to run smoothly and safely also cost more than before, and the men who did the work were both better paid and better protected against dangerously long working hours. Such changes help to explain the growth of operating expenses across the network, from just under half of receipts in the 1860s to nearly two-thirds by the early 1900s. Historians commonly identify this decade as the turning-point in the system's history, even before the First World War inflated costs and stunted investment still further. The cessation of fresh paint layers inside the Midland Grand Hotel hints at a similar story.

In some other countries the picture was very different. In particular the 1900s saw a glorious second flowering of railway architecture in the United States, where early electrification allowed stations such as New York's Grand Central to be rebuilt over the top of newly sunken and smokeless tracks, releasing land for lucrative reuse. Britain's railways, already over-capitalised by the duplication of routes, could afford to electrify only a few suburban lines before 1914, and did not build an all-electric terminus until the 1960s reconstruction of Euston. When major stations were rebuilt in the new century, costly arched train sheds gave way to a revival of the cheaper ridge-and-furrow models, as used in London at Marylebone and in the reconstruction of Charing Cross and Waterloo. Only the last of these could rival the spaciousness of the best arched sheds.

Little of this creeping stagnation was apparent at the time. Those who lived through the decades before the First World War looked back on the railways as impeccably maintained, reliable and financially stable. Though trams and buses had taken away many urban and suburban passengers, motor cars were still an expensive and unreliable novelty, and commercial goods vehicles had yet to offer any serious competition. By comparison with other concerns, the railway companies were also astonishingly large: the Midland alone was valued in 1911 at £120 million, almost seven times more than Imperial Tobacco, the largest non-railway business. While often taken for granted, some lines were also the object of strong loyalty and local pride among staff and passengers. And for all that we may approach a building such as St Pancras armed against false nostalgia, it is hard to look at a photograph like the one opposite without a pang for what has been lost from the experience of travel. At the head of the exquisitely turned-out train is what must be one of the most beautiful machines ever contrived, a Johnson 4-2-2 'Spinner' of 1887. Later trains might be faster and more frequent, but they would never be designed or finished with more care. Here the locomotive and carriages are in crimson lake, a colour that would be adopted for the London, Midland and Scottish Railway after 1923, and would endure into the late 1960s, steadily passing away in favour of the corporate blue-and-white.

By that time inexorable competition from road transport had laid waste much of the nineteenth-century network, and duplicate or under-used routes were closing at a rate of knots. The compensatory fascination for steam locomotives and old trains was also starting to show itself in the now familiar form of redundant lines taken over by volunteers. At these living

27. The 1.30 p.m. Glasgow express waits to leave St Pancras on 2 September 1901. The journey will take around nine hours and more than one change of locomotive. The gleaming 'Spinner' at the head of the train is no. 2601, *Princess of Wales*, one of only two Midland Railway engines to carry a name. Behind is the vast void of Barlow's train shed, with the glazed screen across the end visible above.

museums the hand of the cost-accountant has been stayed, the trains are clean (smuts apart), punctual and graffiti-free, the staff brisk and cheerful. Though the time evoked is now more likely to be the 1950s than the 1900s, the effect is the same: the evocation of a vanished golden age. The paradox is that the apparent stability of the system in its heyday rested on the foundations of a vanquished older world.

CHANGING THE WORLD

The idea of an all-pervading railway revolution is too simplistic to have escaped challenge from transport historians. Even so, their arguments are best understood in terms of qualification. The coming of the railway to a settlement was sometimes followed by mere stagnation or even decline, but mostly it had a stimulating effect. Transport by sea, river and canal remained economically essential, but it did not strike contemporaries as bringing in a new age. Suburban expansion commonly owed more to horse buses, trams, bicycles or simply walking than to trains, but without the railways the process would often have faltered. Horses were never more numerous than when the so-called age of steam was at its zenith, but many of them worked in and out of railway stations and depots. And so on.

Even those Victorians who shunned the trains could not evade the changes they were making, many of which endured long after the railways ceased to be the main carriers of traffic. The very book you are reading, which may have been printed in Surrey or Suffolk, is a case in point. Before the 1860s books published in London were almost always printed there too, as they had been since Caxton's time. Firms in rail-served towns, such as Butler and Tanner's in Frome or Clay's in Bungay, then began to undercut the London print works, and the modern, de-centred book-printing industry took shape.

Food and drink offer further examples. The average British diet in 1900 was very different from what it had been in 1800. Water transport had a lot to do with this: root crops carried along the canal network in the early decades; torrents of cheap overseas grain after Corn Law repeal in the 1840s; frozen meat in refrigerated ships from the New World and Australia towards the century's end. But the origins of the industrial-age diet, at once more varied and more standardised than what came before, lie just as squarely with the railways. The companies themselves did not set out to change the status quo in the kitchen, for heavy goods, minerals and passengers all offered a bigger and surer return. Rather, the network had an enabling effect, allowing canny producers to bypass the limitations of local markets. In this way the swelling population was fed.

First, milk, an extremely perishable commodity even in its pasteurised state. Well into the nineteenth century most of it went to make butter or cheese, which travel and keep better, the residue being consumed as buttermilk or whey. These were the basic dairy commodities of Georgian England, in which milk seems scarcely to have been sold at all in many larger settlements. Other big towns were supplied from small dairy farms around the fringes, while the great cities of London and Liverpool depended on tethered cows kept in back yards and cellars. London alone had 20,000 of these beasts in the 1850s, by which time 'railway milk' from the Home Counties was beginning to offer competition. Then in 1866 most of the Cockney cows perished in a rinderpest epidemic, with impeccable timing from the points of view of the Express Country Milk Supply Company (established 1864) and of the Midland Railway, with its expanding goods depot just beyond St Pancras station. Milk from Derbyshire herds, which was considered unusually long-lasting, was soon streaming down the Midland's line to London, joining the flows into the depots and stations of other lines.

Stimulating production also encouraged specialisation. Large areas of Wiltshire and Berkshire gave up mixed farming for dairying, synchronising their milking times with the railway timetable. By 1900 milk was coming to London from as far away as Cornwall. Consumption of dairy products soared: the average Londoner in 1910 got through the equivalent of nearly half a pint a day, almost four times as much as in 1850. Only the rural market was too scattered and diffuse for effective supply by railway, with the odd result that country folk became some of the biggest customers for condensed milk – delivered to the village, no doubt, by train.

Milk is normally an undifferentiated commodity, but other categories of food are identified by place or style of origin. Cheese is the obvious example, whether named after a county or a village such as Cheddar or Stilton. The last is now produced in the Vale of Belvoir in Leicestershire, near the town of Melton Mowbray. That name brings us to another English staple, the pork pie, and its strange symbiosis with the Midland Railway.

A pork pie can be made by anyone with a supply of pigmeat and pastry, but those of Melton were considered particularly fine. What distinguished them was the 'hand-raised' crust, a free-standing shell that could be filled and baked without being enclosed in a tin. The reputation of this essentially local and fragile delicacy spread rapidly after 1846, when the railway arrived in Melton in the form of a subsidiary route of the Midland system. It helped that the town was also a great centre of fox-hunting, at the junction of the territories of three famous aristocratic hunts. Hunting men had been dogged early opponents of the railway, fearing it would 'grid-iron' the land with impassable barriers. In practice, the new conveyance bolstered the sport by encouraging well-off or socially ambitious townsmen to travel to meets: Anthony Trollope calculated in 1865 that fox-hunting had more than doubled since the trains came.

So the railway at once swelled the number of wealthy visitors who would encounter Melton's famous pies and provided the means for these pies to be sent, securely and in bulk, far beyond the town. Factory production soon supplanted the old household-scale bakers, and by the time the *Daily Telegraph* reported on the phenomenon in 1877 pies were even being dispatched to Paris. The paper's reporter actually missed the connection back to London after the loading of extra pies on to his train delayed its departure, for high-value perishables normally travelled with the passengers rather than on the slower, easily pilfered goods trains. (The Midland used to send out spies in its wagons, hidden under tarpaulins or peeping through eyeholes in the sides, to try to catch the culprits.) The Melton Mowbray pork pie as a distinctive commodity – one that currently seems set to join the élite of EC comestibles of guaranteed regional origin – was thus to a major degree the unwitting creation of the Midland Railway.

Different again from regional specialities are proprietorial foodstuffs: brands, as we would now call them. These seem to have begun around 1800 with bottled sauces and relishes, of which Lea & Perrins (founded 1838) is probably the best-known survival into the modern kitchen cupboard. With the coming of the trains the range of branded foods rapidly expanded, as national markets opened to resourceful local producers. A few big makers killed off numerous small ones; the names of their products joined the common currency of the nation.

The process can be demonstrated by the story of jam. In mid-Victorian times this was still largely made domestically. There was a modest market for cooked and bottled fruit, but most commercial fruit growers could only watch their unmarketable surpluses rot. The transformation of jam into a staple of the working-class home was due to firms such as Messrs Hartley and Messrs Chivers, of whom the latter had the chronological edge. Chivers were based two miles outside Cambridge, at Histon, where market-gardening to supply the university town had taken off in the 1800s. The magic ingredient of the railway followed in 1847: in this case a branch of the Eastern Counties company (later the Great Eastern Railway), which was shared by the Midland's trains. Before long Mr Stephen Chivers, the leading fruit-grower in Histon parish, was using the new line to send produce outside the county. When the glut year 1873 produced more than could be marketed fresh, his sons encouraged him to boil some up for jam instead. A Cambridge grocer stocked the results, which sold very well. So in 1874 Chivers bought land next to Histon station, built a factory on it, and never looked back. By the 1880s the works was also sending out fruit jellies and marmalade; from 1890, bottled fruit; from 1893, preserves in tins. All these processes were housed in a huge complex amid the orchards, in which thousands worked in the peak decades. Other circumstances worked in Chivers's favour, especially the abolition of sugar tax in his start-up year, but it was the presence of the railway that allowed farm to become factory.

Another hidden ingredient in this story is advertising, by which manufacturers such as Chivers sought to create and sustain loyalty to their brands. Advertising in newspapers and periodicals began long before the nineteenth century, but posters were initially restricted to smallish official notices and proclamations. Only in the 1830s and 1840s did big fly-posters begin to smother the walls and hoardings of London. The next stage was the rental of poster sites in return for protection from defacement or covering-over. In the 1840s posters started to appear on the sides of London's horse buses as well. Victorian railway companies never stuck advertisements on the outsides of their beautifully liveried trains – Britain would have to wait until the 1980s for this 'breakthrough' – but with thousands of stations, cuttings, embankments and bridges under their exclusive control they had no need to.

Most Victorians would therefore have encountered large-scale advertising for the first time at a major railway station. As early as 1859 there were complaints that the Midland's station walls in Leicester were being prostituted in this way. In the same year a Birmingham manufacturer called Benjamin Baugh patented his brightly coloured signs of enamelled metal. Unfading, gaudy and robust, these were ideal for railway situations such as retaining walls or the sides of bridges, where bill-stickers could not easily reach. They also suited branded-goods makers, whose products depended on stable and memorable names that warranted permanent advertisement: Fry's chocolate, Mazawattee tea, Wills' cigarettes. Poster design was evolving too: the earliest identified British example in which image and text work together across the whole field dates from 1871. No surprise, then, to learn that advertisements already speckled the walls of St Pancras in 1876, when Williams published his account of the Midland Railway. All that the author could find to say in their defence was that the notices yielded something like £1000 a year for the shareholders (enough to pay the annual wages of a dozen labourers at the London rate). A later Victorian writer on railways, John Pendleton, observed that they had at least not yet climbed 'to the key of the arch'.

Some may find much of this depressingly familiar. The decline of agricultural diversity in favour of intensive specialisation; the divorce of production from consumption; the spread of factory-made foods, trumpeted by intrusive advertising: all have a contemporary ring. The concept of 'food miles' is more recent, as are the associated anxieties about carbon dioxide emissions and climate change. The nineteenth century knew nothing of the last, but the growing dissociation of production from consumption was something that almost everyone in Victorian Britain would have noted and understood.

A short coda to this story can bring us back on to railway territory via the institution of the farmers' market, where consumers buy direct from producers. One of the first of these to open in Britain was in the city of Bath, in 1997. Trading takes place in the redundant train shed of the former Bath Green Park terminus, built by the Midland Railway in 1870 in what had been exclusively Great Western territory. Like its contemporary at St Pancras, the station therefore owes its existence to the company's remorseless expansionism. Another similarity is its division into an architect-designed building facing the street and a glass and iron train shed that was the responsibility of an engineer.

Beyond this point the parallels break down. Bath has a medium-sized and conventionally classical frontage building, meant to harmonise with the city's Georgian inheritance and constructed of local stone rather than St Pancras's system-wide palette of polychromatic materials. Moreover, while St Pancras is set for international stardom, the Midland line to Bath failed to keep a place in the slimmed-down post-war railway network. After closure in 1966 the building sat unused for many years. Then a supermarket was built along-side it, and the train shed was restored for use as its car park. So the train shed now serves the successors of the private cars that effectively killed off the railway, except on Saturdays, when the farmers' market puts up a show of resistance to the supermarket chains. These in their turn are carrying on the standardisation of the food market which the railways them-selves did so much to initiate.

Like the changes to the national diet fostered by the rail-ways, this strange knot of interconnections is a nice illustra-tion of the law of unintended consequences. In a similar way protective legislation has had the unforeseen but widely wel comed effect of keeping major buildings such as Bath station in use for humbler purposes. The mass closure of lines and stations since the 1950s means that examples could easily be multiplied. Yet the surviving network still depends very largely on Victorian buildings, viaducts and tunnels. Unlike (say) the factories or fortifications of the same period, these have proved astonishingly adaptable for the heavier and faster trains and different needs of later generations. St Pancras, which in the 1960s seemed set only for oblivion, is now the subject of the most thoroughgoing and resourceful of these transformations.

7

RESURRECTION

SAVING ST PANCRAS

That St Pancras should become London's international terminus is a remarkable turnaround for a station earmarked
for disposal not very long ago. Its lowest point came in 1966
(the same year that the last trains ran from its classical sibling
station in Bath). What fate the nationalised railway system
then had in mind for St Pancras was not made clear: it
announced merely that the station's future was under review,
together with that of King's Cross. Interim reports suggested
either that King's Cross would be levelled in favour of a combined new station – in which case Barlow's train shed might
be allowed to live on as an exhibition hall or sports centre – or
that the St Pancras train shed might be capable of absorbing
the trains from King's Cross in conjunction with a new concourse building to be erected on the site of the Midland Grand
Hotel. Their vagueness notwithstanding, these threats were
in some ways more ominous than those of the 1930s. Back
then the owning company wanted to rebuild but lacked the
funds; by the 1960s the railways were nationalised, an enormous modernisation plan was under way (involving among
other things the replacement of steam haulage by diesel or
electricity) and large capital projects qualified in Keynesian
terms as praiseworthy public works. It was also intended

that rebuilding would release acres of railway land for public housing, reversing the current that had swept away the slums of Agar Town to make way for St Pancras a century before. Modernisation and public advantage would advance arm in arm across the corpses of St Pancras and King's Cross.

These were not the only differences from the inter-war years. By the 1960s Victorian buildings were increasingly admired, even loved. The letters page of *The Times* in the weeks after the announcement gives an instructive cross-section of opinion. The paper's architectural correspondent had commended the train shed in textbook Functional Tradition terms as a 'forerunner of modern architecture', then raised his game by asserting that the rich and visually poetic hotel was even more worthy of protection. The first published response, a facetiously worded missive from a senior civil servant urging the demolition of both, soon brought other defenders swarming forth. The photographer and architectural historian Eric de Maré used a Ruskinian argument: St Pancras was itself part of history now, a precious embodiment of communal memory. Another correspondent recalled sheltering there from air raids in the company of an elderly London County Council clerk of works, who declared the hotel the finest example of the bricklayer's craft in existence. (Too partial to take seriously was the letter from the vice-chairman of the still extant Butterley iron company, which lauded his company's train shed but declared the hotel too hideous to survive.)

On a wider front, the case for keeping both stations was advanced by the Victorian Society, chaired at that time by Nikolaus Pevsner. The society's best efforts had not been able to save the Euston arch five years before, despite hopes that it could have been relocated elsewhere on the site. The same solution was plainly impossible at St Pancras, which the society argued should be preserved entire as an epitome of 'the greatest period of British history', when the nation was at its zenith of influence and power. Few would have rallied to the cause under this banner in the 1920s or 1930s, when the perception of national decline was less acute. A generation or two later things looked rather different: the Empire that seemed so secure had all but melted away, the industries that had grown up symbiotically with it were struggling against overseas competition, and the policy once dictated independently from Scott's Foreign Office was now bound by the interlocking alliances of the Cold War. The great buildings of Victorian Britain, so confident and optimistic, had become poignant reminders of former glories, like swaggering family portraits squeezed into the commonplace house of a penurious descendant.

The argument from historical significance also side-stepped the misgivings of those who simply didn't *like* the building, especially the hotel. These included Sir John Summerson, whose later denigration of St Pancras was quoted in Chapter 3. Deflecting a request from his old friend Sir John Betjeman that he join with the Victorian Society in its defence, Summerson wrote that he found Scott's design both nauseating and unworthy of special protection. His attitude was representative of many who grew up between the wars, for whom Victorian buildings were too recent to revere and too numerous to cherish, and who looked on the Georgian and industrial traditions as truer bearers of architectural value. A year later, however, Summerson had swallowed his distaste sufficiently to pen a mildly commendatory account of the station for the *Illustrated London News*. The turning-point in its fortunes came a month afterwards, on 2 November 1967, when St Pancras was added to the national list of protected buildings at Grade I: the highest category, of equal rank with Canterbury Cathedral or Windsor Castle.

RE-INVENTING ST PANCRAS

Now that the buildings were secure, plans could be made for their future outside railway ownership. Ideas were canvassed in 1968 at a meeting at Buckingham Palace, chaired by no less a figure than the Duke of Edinburgh. (How proud Scott would have been!) Proposals for the train shed now included an industrial museum, reflecting the burgeoning interest in industrial archaeology. As for the hotel, the Duke's favourite architect, Sir Hugh Casson, had already sketched out a low-budget scheme for conversion to student residences. An alternative project for a return to hotel use was drawn up by Roderick Gradidge, a flamboyant anti-Modernist architect from the Victorian Society's corner. But just as a large hotel company was beginning to nibble, the railways suddenly declared that the station would not now have to close after all.

The events of 1966–8 began with a false alarm and ended like a damp squib, but they also redirected the future history of the site. The buildings now enjoyed the highest level of statutory protection, and as a single entity rather than two detachable units. This guardianship had teeth, too: British Rail got nowhere with its plan of 1978 to junk the panelled wooden ticket office in Scott's booking hall in favour of a modern 'travel centre', even if the Victorian Society had to push the case to a public inquiry to stop it (in the end, the ticket office was simply moved from one wall to another). The next big change was more carefully handled: in 1983 the suburban service to Bedford was electrified, by means of delicate high-tension wires threaded unobtrusively through Barlow's train shed. In terms of usage, however, this was an upward spike on a falling graph. Though St Pancras was still London's station for Nottingham, Derby and Sheffield, services to Manchester, Carlisle and Scotland had become the monopoly of Euston some years before. The beer traffic to the undercroft had gone over to the roads, followed in the 1980s by parcels consignments, once an essential part of every station's business. Then in 1988 suburban trains were redirected through the long-disused tunnel beneath the station, continuing across the centre of London and out on to existing lines on its southern side. In this way a link built primarily to trundle coal through the capital was reborn as part of Thameslink, allowing commuters to shuttle efficiently between Brighton and Bedford and stations between without breaking their journeys. The last office workers moved out of the old Midland Grand in the same year. By 1990 the whole place felt under-used, even half-forgotten.

Beneath this quiet surface things were stirring. As with the 1960s proposals for the area, St Pancras was just one component of a much larger plan, of which only an outline can be given here. Two themes have been constant throughout. One is the vast area of railway goods yards immediately to the north, inherited from the Midland and the Great Northern but largely redundant by the 1980s. Its reuse and reintegration with the fabric of London therefore demanded intelligent planning on a no less giant scale. The other theme is the need to provide an adequate terminus for Continental trains using the new Channel Tunnel. These began running in 1994 to a terminus built along one side of Waterloo station, using existing Victorian-age lines through Kent and inner London. But this arrangement was always meant to be temporary, until a new high-speed line could be built to match those on the Continental side.

The first plan was that the redevelopment of the goods yard would help to underwrite a new underground station, initially meant to burrow below King's Cross, then reassigned to the angle between there and St Pancras. While design work proceeded on this insanely costly option, detailed proposals to revive the hotel were thrashed out in 1987–9. To suit modern expectations of a luxury hotel, the functions were to be rejigged considerably. Bedrooms would be confined to the lower floors, the less spacious storeys within the roof space being converted to apartments. The side wing along Midland Road would become a club open to non-residents, with its own Turkish bath. A luxury shopping arcade would be created within the undercroft, entered directly from the street.

The conversion might well have gone ahead, had it not been for the property slump of the early 1990s. By that time the projected costs of the underground terminus were giving cause for concern, even as the legislation to make it possible was passing through Parliament. A cheaper alternative scheme therefore took its place in 1994: St Pancras itself would become the railway gateway to Europe, and Paris, Lille and Brussels would join Derby, Leicester and Bedford on its destination list. Diving under the Thames near Ebbsfleet, travelling overland across Essex and passing through London mostly by tunnel, the new high-speed connection would be brought to the station across the goods yard site, where space was also available to lay out new connecting spurs to other routes. Another factor in the government's choice of route was the perennial need to regenerate the run-down expanses of East London, for which a new interchange station was proposed at Stratford. A fleet of fast commuter trains to Kent would share the new line, and extra platforms would allow trains for the midlands to continue to use St Pancras too.

The new proposals required the undercroft to be used for access to the platforms above, which was enough to kill off the existing business plan for the hotel's future. None the less, external restoration was carried out in 1993–5, after a structural survey had shown that the building was dropping to bits from neglect. Nine million pounds were spent, painstakingly matching and patching what was missing or damaged, and cleaning the brickwork back to an astonishing orange-red glow, warmer even than that of the new British Library taking shape alongside. The project was a creditable gesture of expiation by British Rail, just before its ideologically minded privatisation and dismemberment. It was also an act of faith that a worthy new use would follow.

Responsibility for that future passed in 1996 to London and Continental Railways, the company constructing the new rail link to the Channel Tunnel. A competition to find a new use for the hotel was won two years later by a consortium made up of the Whitbread Hotel Company in association with Marriott Hotels, and the Manhattan Loft Corporation (despite its name, a British firm specialising in unusual residential conversions). Meanwhile work continued on plans for the station remodelling, taking forward and reshaping earlier designs by the architect Nick Derbyshire that dated from the last years of British Rail. The key names at the railway end are Rail Link Engineering, an international consortium made up of the engineering companies Halcrow and Arup, the project manager Bechtel, the rail consultants Systra and the in-house architectural design team led by Alastair Lansley (working from a masterplan devised earlier by Norman Foster & Partners): a division of labour very different from Victorian practice. Preparations began on site in 2001, using a mixture of public and private funding.

Run the clock forward to 2006, and the following works are in hand. The train shed has been stripped down and re-clad. Its new skin once again follows Barlow's original pattern, with Welsh slate on the lower slopes and a broad band of glazing along the apex (the previous arrangement, with three separate longitudinal strips of glazing, dated from repairs to wartime bomb damage). The framing is now sky-blue: Sir James Allport's preferred colour, which replaced Barlow's dark brown some time in the early 1870s. From 2007 the reconditioned train shed will be entirely given over to Eurostar services to the Continent. The passenger entrance will be through the undercroft, facing a new plaza that is being created in the angle between St Pancras and King's Cross. Arrivals, departures, customs and the like will be dealt with amid the iron colonnades of this lower level, which will be ventilated by means of ducts in a newly laid floor. Escalators rising through four big slots cut into Barlow's platform deck will take passengers to and from the trains. A new concrete floor or raft has been laid at this upper level to secure the structure, allowing Barlow's cross-girders to be cut through without destabilising the iron arches overhead. The platforms, now six in

28. A computer image of the train-shed interior converted for Eurostar
services. Broad slots are cut into the floor, both for escalator access and to
allow natural light into the basement. The train-shed roof is shown more
extensively glazed than in Barlow's time – compare p. 75.

number, have also been completely replanned: a final vindication of Barlow's column-free, flexible interior. Such changes have entailed significant losses to the original fabric, but the company also points out that the new entrance route will expose and explain Barlow's structure in ways not normally apparent before. So the station will become a kind of reincarnation of itself: more self-conscious than before, certainly, but decidedly alive and of the present day.

The Victorian train shed is far too short for the enormously long Continental trains, so the six new platforms extend a long way beyond it. Next to these extensions on the east side, beyond the old train shed, are three additional new platforms for the high-speed Kent commuter trains; next to them on the west are four more platforms for diesel trains operating the midlands-bound services for which the station was first built. (The latest exhumations from St Pancras's churchyard were to make way for the approach to the latter.) These extra platform areas rest on a very large substructure and are sheltered by a new train-shed extension. Lower and much wider than Barlow's, this is also of deliberately contrasting form: flat-topped and straight-sided, with simple steel colonnades inside, and glazed north-facing slots in the roof for natural light. The entire addition was built in phases without interrupting normal services. It joins the old train shed by means of a cross-concourse under a separate type of glazing, which can be entered at street level or by escalator from a new Underground ticket hall. Beyond this point the new structure extends, in the words of its architect, 'like a flying carpet'. This clear separation of new and old fabric is a familiar principle of design when historic buildings are adapted – an in-joke refers to that busy architect Frank

29. The train-shed extension in 2005, when half-complete. The shelter and the glazed concourse separating it from Barlow's train shed have since been extended across the full width.

Juxtaposition – but here it also echoes the way Barlow's train shed stops short against the back of Scott's hotel. How well the frank juxtaposition will work in aesthetic terms must wait until the works are finally complete, when the view outwards from within Barlow's train shed will be the key.

Other essential works are buried below ground, as in the 1860s. The key improvement is a new station for the Thameslink trains, built alongside the western perimeter of the old station on the site of some lesser offices sacrificed for the purpose. It was constructed by means of a method introduced to the capital for the Jubilee Line tube extension in the 1990s, which can serve as a representative example of the ingenuity and tenacity of the modern civil engineer. Piles were first sunk on either side of the original tunnel. These were capped with beams and topped with a slab roof. The giant box thus created was then excavated by means of equipment lowered in through holes in the new roof, and a new tunnel constructed inside. When this void is fully fitted out, the cramped existing station a little way down the line – recently notorious as the arrival point of the four suicide bombers of 7 July 2005 – can be closed. The terrace under the access ramp in front of the hotel has also been excavated, as part of a new and immensely costly concourse to the Underground station shared between St Pancras and King's Cross. As completed in summer 2006, this features new red-brick facing with Scott-style Gothic motifs along the inner side, where the space comes up against the hotel foundations, giving the nice illusion of freshly exposed Victorian fabric.

Work to convert the hotel did not begin until the same year, and so is less advanced at the time of writing. Manhattan Lofts have now taken over direction of the project, with

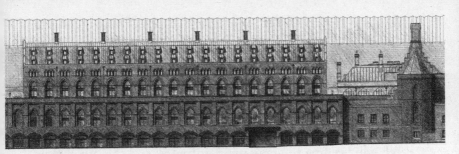

West (Midland Road) Elevation

30. Most of the new hotel rooms will be in this new extension, built over
the reconstructed Thameslink station along the west side of the train shed
(visible behind). The façade by Richard Griffiths Architects echoes motifs
from Scott's building, part of which appears on the right.

Marriott Hotels as the operating partner. Their architects are RHWL, working with Richard Griffiths Architects as conservation architects. As in the 1980s plan, the two roof storeys are to become private apartments, along with parts of two other floors, to a total of sixty-eight. The hotel will take the rest, including some spaces on the railway side made redundant by the undercroft conversion. So the departures arch will become the new main entrance, and the cab shelter beyond it will re-emerge as a giant top-glazed lounge, not unlike the palm courts that came into fashion for hotels a decade or so after Midland Grand was completed. The booking hall immediately alongside will become a dining room, and the original entrance hall at the end of the crescent wing will be reborn as a bar. A new wing is also to be built to raise the tally of bedrooms to 244, large enough to sustain the facilities required for a five-star hotel. This will sit on top of the Thameslink station box on the west side, resting on rubber pads to cushion its occupants from vibration. So that it reads unmistakably as part of the hotel, Richard Griffiths Architects have designed the façade with pointed-headed arches set in red brick.

Inside, difficult decisions are being made as to how far, if at all, the nineteenth-century decoration will be re-created. Much of the first decorative treatment survives, hidden under later treatments and topped by the plain paint layers of the twentieth century. There are also many scars from drillings-in, patchings-over and modifications for office use. To scrape back to the founding treatment, in the manner of archaeologists recovering a medieval wall painting from under white-wash, would therefore show up something far too patched and damaged to suit a luxury hotel. It would also take years and cost millions. Nor is there much hope of recovering more than a few pieces of Gillows' original furniture, or much point in trying to refabricate it from drawings and photographs. So the likeliest solution is a mixture of re-created decoration, new schemes and the selected preservation of samples of old work, with new furniture in keeping. Redundant or obsolete servicing will be sacrificed only after a thorough record has been made.

Scott would have recognised these challenges, which are similar to those he faced when restoring a great cathedral. His declared solution in such cases was to preserve as much old fabric as possible and to design new work in harmony with what he considered the spirit of the building. For all that his practice often fell short of his theory, he was surely on the right lines. By this line of descent, something of the spirit of the Gothic Revival may infuse the rejuvenated Midland Grand Hotel, even if Gothic-Revival-Revival may be a better label for its new addition.

This is not the whole story of the changes afoot in this corner of London, N1. It leaves out the reconstruction of the concourse at King's Cross; the plans for the vast goods yard site, claimed to be the largest inner-city regeneration project in Western Europe, and its remaining historic structures; the dismantling and selective reassembly of the Victorian gasholders that stood as unforgettable landmarks just outside St Pancras; the ecological assessment of the works, and the measures taken to protect scarce species that have recolonised the old industrial sites; and so on. Likewise, it glosses over the detailed succession of plans and designs along the way, which could easily fill a book in themselves. The length and complexity of this story owe much to the requirement that the station should stay in use for normal services throughout its chrysalis years and still more to the stringency of modern planning controls and historic buildings legislation. However drastic some of these changes, the painstaking transformation of St Pancras therefore also reflects the values we now invest in our own inheritance from the past.

LEAVING ST PANCRAS

The Victorians were the first to confront the idea of unrelenting change as the normal state of things, whether in industry, agriculture, communication, scientific knowledge or religious belief. Though Victorian culture repeatedly framed itself in terms of the past, it therefore stressed that the present state of things was necessarily different, whether for good or ill. Two book titles of the 1840s sound the keynote for the epoch: Thomas Carlyle's *Past and Present* and John Henry Newman's *Loss and Gain*. Or there is Tennyson's bracing line from 'Locksley Hall', written not long after the poet witnessed the infant Liverpool and Manchester Railway at work: 'Let the great world spin forever down the ringing grooves of change' (he later apologised for having misunderstood the distinction between grooves and rails, owing in part to his having visited after dark). For their part, the new railway companies sought an accommodation with established culture by means of their quasi-military staff uniforms, heraldic borrowings, smart carriage liveries like those of the nobility and – of course – their architecture. Scott's Midland Grand Hotel, with its mature and intelligent fusion of ancient and modern motifs, epitomises this attempt to reconcile past and present.

In turn, a modern journey from the station allows a kind

of dialogue with the past, and some reflections on our own layered and interconnected world. Some of the changes are unmissable: the Eurostar route passes through modern London's biggest reconstruction areas, including the goods yard, the interchange station and Olympic zone at Stratford and the proposed Thames Gateway growth area. Yet many believe that climate change and rising waters may shortly make much of the last uninhabitable, just as ideas of catastrophic inundation dominated early Victorian geology, and just as Ruskin's last years were haunted by visions of catastrophic pollution, 'The Storm-Cloud of the Nineteenth Century'. The line also passes relics of a more rooted culture, such as the diminutive Norman church of Newington village just before the tunnel entrance at Folkestone, a rural counterpart to Old St Pancras at the start of the journey. On the hillside nearby is a recent chalk-cut figure of a giant horse, the latest contribution to a southern English tradition that can be traced back to the White Horse made by late Bronze Age peoples at Uffington in present-day Oxfordshire: a self-conscious attempt at negotiation between antiquity and today. The security measures taken to prevent asylum-seekers from jumping the incoming trains can stand a reminder of the tribal divisions of our own time.

When the view from the window palls, travellers can retreat into virtual worlds via their MP3 players and laptops, or bounce texts, speech and images around the globe by mobile phone. Some will celebrate these innovations as a liberation from constraints of time and space, a second revolution to match the railways' abolition of distance. Others may lament the decline of reading, writing and polite conversation with strangers, which passed the time for older generations of travellers. A few thoughts on the rigours of railway travel before proper heating, buffet cars or lavatories, or on the justifiable anxieties that beset unaccompanied women travelling in isolated compartments, and the picture changes again. By attempting in such ways to deal justly with the past, as we may hope that posterity will deal justly with us, we reoccupy positions mapped out by our Victorian forebears.

Beyond that, the reader must take over. All that might be added by way of farewell is that a railway journey can still foster this sense of layering and interconnectedness, as the city-dodging blur of the motorway, the pressurised bubble of the airliner and the air-conditioned nowhere that is the international airport generally do not. And that St Pancras station is architecturally the finest place to start or finish such a journey in Britain, and perhaps the finest anywhere: a wonder of the world.

FURTHER READING

The standard work, which was also the first modern monograph on any of Britain's Victorian buildings, is Jack Simmons, *St Pancras Station* (1968). This outstanding book, by the most thoughtful and acute of British railway historians, was excellently revised and updated by Robert Thorne in 2003. Thorne also co-edited *Change at King's Cross* (1990, with Michael Hunter), which has much of additional interest on St Pancras, the goods yard, and the area around. Charles E. Lee, *St Pancras Church and Parish* (1955), tells the longer story of the urban surroundings, and Phil Emery summarises the recent excavations in *British Archaeology* 88 (May/June 2006); a monograph is also forthcoming. Barlow's account of his own train shed is in the *Minutes of the Proceedings of the Institution of Civil Engineers*, vol. 30 (1869–70); the best contemporary descriptions of the hotel are in the *Building News* (22 May 1874). Substantial later articles on the station include that by Dan Cruickshank in the *Architect's Journal* (20 November 1997), which must be treated with caution where the staircase is concerned, and Gilbert Herbert, 'St Pancras Reconsidered: A Case Study in the Interface of Architecture and Engineering', in *The Journal of Architecture and Planning Research*, 15/3 (1998), which explains the relationship between Scott's design and Barlow's overall plan. Sir John Summerson's case against St Pancras is put most forcefully in his *Victorian Architecture: Four Studies in Evaluation* (Columbia University Press, 1970), that of the *Quarterly Review* in vol. 264 (April 1872).

SCOTT AND THE GOTHIC REVIVAL

Chris Brooks, *The Gothic Revival* (Phaidon *Art and Ideas* series, 1999), is the best general account, and lavishly illustrated in colour. The identically titled book of 2002 by Michael J. Lewis in Thames and Hudson's *World of Art* series is less substantial but strong on Continental themes. Both have good outline bibliographies. Kenneth Clark, *The Gothic Revival: An Episode in the History of Taste* (1928, several reissues), can still be read with pleasure for its aphoristic Twenties qualities. The pioneering survey is C. L. Eastlake, *A History of the Gothic Revival* (1872; reissued edition by J. Mordaunt Crook, 1970). More general works on the period include Roger Dixon and Stefan Muthesius, *Victorian Architecture* (*World of Art* series, 1978; second edition 1985), and Henry-Russell Hitchcock, *Architecture: Nineteenth and Twentieth Centuries* (*Pelican History of Art*, fourth edition, 1977). Peter Collins, *Changing Ideals in Modern Architecture 1750–1950* (1965), sets out the theoretical basis of Modernism; Nikolaus Pevsner, *Some Architectural Writers of the Nineteenth Century*, explores the more diverse literature that came before it.

George Gilbert Scott has yet to receive a full biography, a daunting assignment for any human lifetime. While we wait, David Cole, *The Work of Sir Gilbert Scott* (1980), is a sound introductory account. Scott's *Remarks on Secular and Domestic Architecture* (1857) is inevitably scarce outside major libraries, but his *Personal and Professional Recollections* have been edited by Gavin Stamp and reissued with much previously unpublished material (1995). Stamp's life of George Gilbert Scott junior, *An Architect of Promise* (2002), also has valuable material on the elder Scott (as well as on the turn away from Neo-Gothic), as do the memoirs of Scott's pupil T. G. Jackson, likewise reissued in an enhanced edition, as *Recollections: The Life and Travels of a Victorian Architect* (2003, editor Sir Nicholas Jackson). Scott's other great secular commissions are covered in monographs: *The Albert Memorial* (2000), edited by Chris Brooks, and Ian Toplis, *The Foreign Office: An Architectural History* (1987). Drawings by the Scott family held in the RIBA collection have their own volume in its published catalogue (1981). A new biography of Pugin, by Rosemary Hill, is in preparation; facsimiles of his *Contrasts*, *True Principles* and other books have been published more than once. For latter-day devotees there is a Pugin Society, whose journal is also called *True Principles*. The standard account of the Cambridge Camden Society is James F. White, *The Cambridge Movement* (1962), supplemented by the essays in Christopher Webster and John Elliott (editors), *'A Church As It Should Be': The Cambridge Camden Society and Its Influence* (2000). Ruskin's influence on architecture is assessed in Michael W. Brooks, *John Ruskin and Victorian Architecture* (1989), and the conference papers edited by Rebecca Daniels and Geoff Brandwood, *Ruskin and Architecture* (2003); that of Morris in Chris Miele (ed.), *From William Morris* (Yale University Press, *Studies in British Art*, 14, 2005). Elizabeth Cumming and Wendy Kaplan, *The Arts and Crafts Movement* (1991), is a good general introduction to wider issues of design.

Carroll L. V. Meeks, *The Railroad Station: An Architectural History* (New Haven, 1956), addresses most of the main themes on the architectural side. Jeffrey Richards and John M. Mackenzie, *The Railway Station: A Social History* (1986), puts flesh on the architectural bones. Steven Parissien's spectacularly illustrated *Station to Station* (1997) is also refreshingly cosmopolitan in approach. Specifically British surveys include Marcus Binney and David Pearce (editors), *Railway Architecture* (SAVE Britain's Heritage, 1979), and Gordon Biddle, *Victorian Stations* (1973). *Britain's Historic Railway Structures* (2003), by the last-named author, includes a scholarly gazetteer of all the country's listed railway structures. For the London story, Alan A. Jackson, *London's Termini* (1969), remains a standard work, and John Betjeman and John Gay, *London's Historic Railway Stations* (1972), is good fun. Shorter but more up-to-date descriptions can be found in the London volumes of the *Buildings of England* series (Pevsner Architectural Guides). Paddington now has an excellent monograph by Steven Brindle (English Heritage, 2004), who has also written the biography *Brunel: The Man Who Built the World* (2005). A concise biography of Barlow is included in the new *Oxford Dictionary of National Biography*. For Newcastle, see John Addyman and Bill Fawcett, *The High Level Bridge and Newcastle Central Station: 150 Years across the Tyne* (1999). V. R. Anderson and G. K. Fox, *Midland Railway Architecture* (1985), is self-explanatory.

Far less has been published on hotels. Nikolaus Pevsner, *A History of Building Types* (1976), sketches the outline of development. Derek Taylor and David Bush, *The Golden Age of British Hotels* (1974), is lively but unreliable; Oliver Carter,

British Railway Hotels 1838–1983 (1990), is both more special-ised and more accurate. Blanchard Jerrold's East End tour is from his *London: A Pilgrimage* (1872; reissued 1970 and since). A general bibliography of British architecture is available on-line at the Pevsner Architectural Guides' educational website, *www.lookingatbuildings.org.uk*.

TRAINS AND RAILWAYS

The literature on railways is vast, much of it British, and much of that pictorial or nostalgic in character. Substantial and complementary narratives of the building of St Pancras can be found in the histories of the Midland Railway by Frederick Williams (*The Midland Railway: Its Rise and Progress*, 1876; facsimile edition 1968) and the two volumes by E. G. Barnes (*The Rise of the Midland Railway, 1844–1874* and *The Midland Main Line, 1875–1922*, 1966 and 1969). The administrative and financial background to the London extension is ana-lysed by Geoffrey Cannon in the *Economic History Review*, second series, 25 (1972). A shorter account is *The Midland Railway: A New History* (1988); John Gough, *The Midland Railway: A Chronology* (1989), is a comprehensive survey of the system. C. Hamilton Ellis, *The Midland Railway* (1953), can be recommended to the locomotive-minded. Other detailed studies include R. E. Lacy and George Dow's two volumes, *Midland Railway Carriages* (1984 and 1986), and two as yet incomplete multi-volume accounts of its locomotives, by Stephen Summerson (Irwell Press) and R. J. Essery and David Jenkinson (Wild Swan). George Dow, *Midland Style* (1975), covers liveries, uniforms and the like. The Midland Railway Society publishes a *Journal* and the more occasional

Midland Record. There is also a Midland Railway Study Centre, located at the Silk Mill industrial museum at Derby, where collections of ceramics, ephemera etc. are held.

For general themes the best place to start is Jack Simmons and Gordon Biddle's encyclopaedic *Oxford Companion to British Railway History* (1999). Of thematic accounts, two studies by Simmons stand near the head of the list: *The Victorian Railway* (1991) and *The Railway in Town and Country 1830–1914* (1986). Michael J. Freeman, *Railways and the Victorian Imagination* (1999), includes some interesting reinterpretations. The same author has edited *Transport in Victorian Britain* (1988, with Derek H. Aldcroft), which sets the iron road in context. J. R. Kellett, *The Impact of Railways on Victorian Cities* (1969), assesses the urban aspects. Of older accounts, W. M. Acworth, *The Railways of England* (1889; fifth edition 1900), stands out: written by a journalist whose critical attitude softened as he came to understand his subject, and dedicated to 'The Three Hundred Thousand Servants of the Public'. How the network grew is described in detail in the fifteen-volume series published by David & Charles, *A Regional History of the Railways of Great Britain* (1960–89). The milk story is told by P. J. Atkins in the *Journal of Transport History*, 4 (1978), the pork pie story by J. E. Brownlow in *Transactions of the Leicester Archaeological and Historical Society*, 39 (1963–4), the Chivers jam story in vol. 9 of the *Victoria County History* for Cambridgeshire (1989), the advertising story in E. S. Turner, *The Shocking History of Advertising!* (1952), and T. R. Nevett, *Advertising in Britain* (1982).

The works for the new high-speed line are described in the *Railway Magazine* vol. 151 (June and July 2005).

LIST OF ILLUSTRATIONS

ILLUSTRATION CREDITS

1, 10, Crown Copyright, National Monuments Record; 4, courtesy of *Private Eye*; 6, 11, courtesy of Gavin Stamp; 8, A. F. Kersting; 14, 22, Science and Society Picture Library; 15, courtesy of *The Railway Magazine*; 16a, Birmingham City Archives, John Whybrow Collection; 20, courtesy of Emap Communications Ltd; 21, Janet Hall/RIBA Library Photographs Collection; 24, Aberdeen Art Gallery & Museums Collections; 27, courtesy of LCGB, Ken Nunn Collection; 28, courtesy of London & Continental Railways; 29, *Guardian*; 30, courtesy of Richard Griffiths Architects

ACKNOWLEDGEMENTS

First thanks are due to my editors Mary Beard and Peter Carson for commissioning a book covering three long-standing enthusiasms – railways, the history of London, and the Gothic Revival – and also to Andrew Franklin at Profile Books for his support and enthusiasm. Early drafts were read by Zoe Croad of English Heritage, by Robert Thorne and William Filmer-Sankey of Alan Baxter Associates, by Richard Hill of Richard Griffiths Architects, and by Phil Emery, Andrew Saint, Gavin Stamp, Royden Stock and Gavin Watson, all of whom generously shared their knowledge and ideas. Gavin Stamp also lent historic items for reproduction, as did John Minnis. Finally I must thank my father for my first trip to St Pancras, train-watching on a chill April day in 1977.

INDEX

WONDERS OF THE WORLD

This is a small series of books that will focus on some of the world's most famous sites or monuments. Their names will be familiar to almost everyone: they have achieved iconic stature and are loaded with a fair amount of mythological baggage. These monuments have been the subject of many books over the centuries, but our aim, through the skill and stature of the writers, is to get something much more enlightening, stimulating, even controversial, than straightforward histories or guides. The series is under the general editorship of Mary Beard. Other titles in the series are:

Published
Mary Beard: **The Parthenon**
Cathy Gere: **The Tomb of Agamemnon**
Simon Goldhill: **The Temple of Jerusalem**
Keith Hopkins & Mary Beard: **The Colosseum**
Robert Irwin: **The Alhambra**
Richard Jenkyns: **Westminster Abbey**
Keith Miller: **St Peter's**
John Ray: **The Rosetta Stone**
Gavin Stamp: **The Memorial to the Missing of the Somme**

Unpublished
Geremie Barmé & Bruce Doar: **The Forbidden City**
Iain Fenlon: **St Mark's Square**
Rosemary Hill: **Stonehenge**
Giles Tillotson: **Taj Mahal**
David Watkin: **The Roman Forum**